THE FRONT LINE

A PRAYER WARRIOR'S GUIDE TO SPIRITUAL BATTLE

THE FRONT LINE

JOHN BORNSCHEIN

WITH DAVID BUTTS, KATHY BRANZELL, AND DION ELMORE

KIRKDALE PRESS

The Front Line: A Prayer Warrior's Guide to Spiritual Battle

Copyright 2012 John Bornschein.

Kirkdale Press, 1313 Commercial St., Bellingham, WA 98225
http://kirkdalepress.com

ISBN 978-1-57-799534-0
Ebook ISBN 978-1-57799-513-5

Cover Design: Quintin Cooke
Typesetting: projectluz.com

After they prayed, the place where they were meeting was shaken. And they were all filled with the Holy Spirit and spoke the word of God boldly.

—Acts 4:31

CONTENTS

ABBREVIATIONS

AMP   The Amplified Bible

KJV   King James Version

NASB   New American Standard Bible

NIV   New International Version

NKJV   New King James Version

INTRODUCTION

At this point, you have probably picked up a book or two on prayer. Perhaps dialogue with the Almighty is something that you are seeking to learn more about, and deep down you know you've only scratched the surface. Well, you have taken a bold step. This book will both challenge and empower you, and through the journey, you will gain a greater understanding of the weapons of our warfare on the spiritual battlefield.

The front line is the threshold where the battle is won or lost. It is the turning point for victory or defeat, where the will of the mind prevails over flesh through faith and the empowering of the Holy Spirit. Just as Gideon and his 300 warriors stood firm in the face of the enemy, we must be bold for truth in a society of moral relativism. Courage under fire requires a necessary balance of prayer and Scripture study within the church body—harmony between order and discipline. It is the fortitude of knowledge and unity to bring down barriers and move mountains in our culture.

Preparation for battle requires advanced training for men and women of faith. Scripture tells us that "Anyone who lives on milk, being still an infant, is not acquainted with the teaching about righteousness. But solid food is for the mature, who by constant use have trained themselves to distinguish good from evil" (Heb 5:13–14). The battlefield is real, and the devil is very aware of you. In fact, he is a roaring lion looking for someone to devour (1 Pet 5:8), and he has you in his sights. Why? Because if you are a Christian, you are a child of the living God. You have power that the human mind cannot fully comprehend, and this power is unleashed through prayer. The adversary knows your potential, and he will stop at nothing to prevent you from accomplishing your mission here on earth. He will strike at every area of your life to bring you down. But "count it all joy" (Jas 1:2 NKJV), for once you know what the devil knows about who you are in Christ Jesus, you will stand boldly at the front lines, seeing only victory, not defeat.

The authors who contributed to this resource have spent decades studying prayer in depth and have compiled this book as a field manual to prepare you for spiritual warfare. The battlefield is multidimensional and must be fought on several fronts. There are times to get your hands dirty and there are times to get your knees dirty. On your knees, you will wage a war that is not bound by the borders of the sea, air, or land. These battles must be fought simultaneously, for physical strongholds are spiritually sustained one way or another. In the art of war, you do not strike the enemy from one side alone; you must employ a multifaceted strategy, attacking the enemy from all sides.

The dominion of darkness is at work all over our planet with the sole purpose of destroying humankind and taking the birthright that is freely given to those who accept the gift to be heirs of the Most High. The armies of our adversary know who the soldiers of the kingdom are, and they know those who are not (Acts 19:13–16). They are also afraid and know their time is short (Jas 2:18–19; Rev 12:12).

Right now, you may be willing to jump into the fight and build a lasting legacy that will never erode and has eternal blessing. That is honorable. However, before you can walk in the Valley of Elah and take on Goliath, you must be trained in the discipline of spiritual warfare. To be a true prayer warrior is the highest, most effective level a combatant in the kingdom can attain. Everything done under the heavens is accomplished through prayer. Nothing will stand against the forces of evil without it.

An incredible connection is formed between believers and the heavenly Father during prayer. This connection is something that intersects the physical with the spiritual and goes far beyond human comprehension. The ability for humankind to speak in the throne room of the Almighty is awesome in and of itself. But the fact that God in all of His splendor will stop and listen intently to our every word, as if nothing could be more important to Him at that moment, is truly breathtaking. God desires relationship with us, and our dialogue with Him through prayer is where He reveals the deepest characteristics of His nature. In the book of Philippians, the Apostle Paul reminds us that our determined purpose is to become more deeply and intimately acquainted with God. There is great power in this fellowship.

You have been called for such a time as this to be a light in a dark world. I challenge you now to continue your training and learn what real hand-to-hand combat is all about.

CHAPTER ONE

CALL TO WAR

JOHN BORNSCHEIN

I n the powerful work, *Giving Ourselves to Prayer*, Gary T. Meadors observes that dialogue with the Almighty is part of the fabric of the Bible: "Genesis 4:26 first mentions that 'men began to call on the name of the Lord,' and Revelation 22:20 closes the Bible with the prayer, 'Come, Lord Jesus' (compare 1 Cor 16:22). The entire history of redemption is framed in prayer. In between these terminal references we find a database about prayer that is so large it requires description beyond simple definition."[1] Why do we pray? Here are a few key reasons:[2]

1. **We love Him.** Just as a man and woman in love desire to be together and communicate, so we, if we love God, will desire to be with Him and to fellowship with Him in proportion to our love for Him.

2. **We depend on God. He is our source.** He is our life (Col 3:4). Through prayer, we receive the comfort, strength, and all the other resources we need in life, both naturally and spiritually. Prayer—relationship with God—is as necessary to the spiritual life as air is to the natural life.

3. **Prayer allows us to resist temptation.** Jesus warned His disciples to "watch and pray, lest you enter into temptation" (Matt 26:41 NKJV). Living a life without prayer can leave us weak and exposed, giving an opportunity for the enemy to gain ground and potentially lure us into sin.

4. **Prayer is necessary for people to invite God to act in salvation.** God gave the earth to Adam and his descendants, so we must invite God to work here. If no one invites Him to work on earth, Satan—the "god of this age" because of humanity's universal rebellion (2 Cor 4:4)—will dominate human affairs, and eventually the judgment of God will come. By inviting God to intercede often and specifically, multitudes can be saved who would otherwise be lost.

5. **God commands us to pray.** In Colossians 4:2, Paul writes: "Continue earnestly in prayer, being vigilant in it with thanksgiving" (NKJV). Jesus also encouraged His followers to pray: "Then He [Jesus] spoke a parable to them, that men always ought to pray and not lose heart" (Luke 18:1 NKJV).

The need to pray is as great as the authority of God, who commands us to "pray without ceasing" (1 Thess 5:17 NKJV). Prayer is so vital to all that God wants to do on the earth, and it is so essential to us, that He commands us to do it all the time. We should even deny ourselves sleep and food at times to pray more and with greater power (see Matt 6:16; Luke 6:12; 21:36; Col 4:2; 2 Cor 11:27). Or, as John Chrysostom wrote:

> Prayer has subdued the strength of fire. It has bridled the rage of lions, hushed anarchy to rest, extinguished wars, appeased the elements, burst the chains of death,

expanded the fates of heaven, assuaged diseases, dispelled frauds, rescued cities from destruction, staid the sun in its course, and arrested the progress of the thunderbolt. In this communion with God, there is an all-sufficient panoply, a treasure undiminished, a mine that is never exhausted, a sky unobscured by clouds, a heaven unruffled by the storm. It is the root, the fountain, the mother of a thousand blessings![3]

Using information gleaned from a 2008 poll about spirituality in America, *Parade Magazine* noted that: "Our nation was built on a foundation of strong faith, and in some respects, that hasn't changed." The poll found that "69% of Americans believe in God, 77% pray outside of religious services, and 75% believe it's a parent's responsibility to give children a religious upbringing." In contrast to speculation that "a new atheism" is at rise in the U.S., this study found that "only 5% of respondents didn't believe in God. ... [In fact,] 67% said they pray because it brings them comfort and hope."[4]

The National Day of Prayer Task Force, where I serve as executive director, began calling the nation to prayer in 1991 under the leadership of Mrs. Shirley Dobson. As millions gathered each year in solemn assembly asking the Lord to intervene in America, He answered in numerous ways. We can't directly tie declines in negative cultural statistics to prayer, but the timing is certainly worth taking note of. Between 1994 and 2008, the violent crime rate in America decreased 17.7 percent, and the property crime rate decreased 19.5 percent.[5]

The role of prayer in America cannot be ignored. Jennifer Harper of the *Washington Times* writes, "Politicians come and go, fashions evolve and the culture shifts with alarming frequency. One thing remains constant, though. Americans pray. A lot. Ninety percent have a spiritual interlude with God every day, according to a study released Thursday by Brandeis University. Half pray several times a day, in fact."[6]

The National Day of Prayer website has cited numerous stories of answered prayers that have made headline news across the country, including the following report published by the task force in 2009:

> In big cities and small towns, Christians are using their faith and prayers to combat crime, homelessness, corruption and economic doldrums.
>
> Following a forty-day prayer vigil organized by the Orlando Police Department, a dramatic decrease in crime was reported. The goal was to reduce crime in Orlando by taking God's word outside of churches and onto the streets. "We want to come to the street and bring the love and the compassion of our lord, Jesus Christ, to the community," said Angel Torres, an Orlando Police Department chaplain.[7]

The report goes on to detail similar cases of answered prayers in communities, including Washington, D.C.; Manchester, Kentucky; and "[d]ozens of towns, from Georgia to Texas."

We have seen other major victories through prayer. In 2008, Proposition 8 was upheld in California and marriage was protected. Recently, the words "In God We Trust" were etched back into the new Capitol Visitor Center. And through the tireless efforts of citizens submitting petitions, as well as the diligent work of the Alliance Defense Fund and WallBuilders, concerted efforts to strip away the faith of this nation have been repeatedly thwarted. But the opponents of faith won't stay silent. Even so, the National Day of Prayer has persevered despite several lawsuits from non-Christian organizations.

The voice of the saints cannot be ignored.

Without prayer, none of these victories would have been won. Before Proposition 8 went to a vote in California, tens of thousands filled Qualcomm Stadium in San Diego to fast and pray in support of traditional marriage.[8] And when the National Day of Prayer became the subject of a federal lawsuit, more than 250,000 people joined together via social networks to pray.[9] The victories belong to God, but the body of Christ knew they had to act in faith, lifting each matter before Him and seeking His intervention.

Millions of people gathered across the world on the Global Day of Prayer, and more than one million believers marched through the streets of Mexico City, shouting praises to the Lord while they fasted and prayed. Between 2008 and 2010, more than 700,000 Americans filled stadiums to pray in over a dozen states,[10] while 24-hour houses of prayer began springing up across the county. According to some estimates, more than three million people gathered on the National Day of Prayer, making it the largest designated day of prayer in the world.[11] The Prayer Movement is alive and well, gaining momentum as never before.

DOES PRAYER WORK?

Prayer is making a difference, transforming the landscape of homes and communities across the globe. In 1999, Heritage Builders conducted an unofficial study of the American family to determine the factors that increased overall family health. What they discovered was truly incredible. A summary of their findings indicated that families who ate together at least four days a week and prayed at the dinner table showed the highest percentage of honor roll students and church-attending teenagers between the ages of 15 and 19.[12]

A Lifeway Research survey estimates that 70 percent of Christian teens and young adults will walk away from the Church during college.[13] But families that prayed together were among the 30 percent whose teenagers were more grounded in their faith.[14] In the Lifeway survey, participants indicated that prayer was not just a part of religious practice; rather, it was the concerted effort of parents making sure that prayer was emphasized in daily living, not simply as a response to life's trials and tribulations. Even secular universities agree that prayer makes a difference in relationships.

You may have heard the saying, "A couple that prays together, stays together." Although we know this to be true, it is helpful to examine the evidence that best supports this common perception. An article published in the *Journal of Social and Clinical Psychology* had this to say about prayer: "There is some evidence that religiosity is similarly related to several positive relationship outcomes. Specifically, greater involvement in religious activities [including prayer] is related to higher levels of marital satisfaction ... and marital stability with three longitudinal studies indicating that religiousness predicts lower risk of divorce and divorce proneness."[15]

The report goes on to cite that "prayer may help couples to more often 'think of the needs of others, be more loving and forgiving, treat each other with respect, and resolve conflict.' " The researchers suggest that the relationship people experience with God through prayer helps them handle their emotions, be more empathetic, become less self-focused, and gain greater skills in reconciliation. They also note that "prayer for the partner might prime partners to think about each other in more loving or compassionate terms and so treat each other with greater respect and sensitivity."[16]

Praying regularly together also "helped couples prevent conflict in their relationships." Researchers note that couples who included "God in their marriage through prayer" were more skilled in problem solving and reconciliation. Other couples "reported that prayer alleviated tension and facilitated open communication during conflict."

BEYOND THE HOME

Even if God didn't answer the prayers of His people, according to research, the positive effects of prayer are undeniable. When a father prays for his children, what is he demonstrating in that action? He is showing them true humility, compassion, and love. He is also showing that he is accountable to someone bigger than himself and that there is a structured chain of command that keeps the family healthy and aligned.

A 1997 survey revealed that 93 percent of women wanted their husbands to take on the spiritual leadership of the home.[17] These same women indicated that they would give greater respect and support to their husbands if they demonstrated more effort to lead in this area. Now, let me ask you: if women respected their husbands more because they were taking the lead in prayer at home, would this not have a positive impact on the overall health of families?

With this in mind, imagine what the action of prayer does for a community. If religious leaders are praying for civil leaders, they are honoring that which God has put in place. As Romans 13:1 states, "Let everyone be subject to the governing authorities, for there is no authority except that which God has established." Paul also encouraged believers to pray for their leaders: "I urge … that petitions, prayers, intercession and thanksgiving be made for all people—for kings and all those in authority, that we may live peaceful and quiet lives in all godliness and holiness. This is good, and pleases God our Savior, who wants all people to be saved and to come to a knowledge of the truth" (1 Tim 2:1–4).

A nation can be punished by the actions of its leaders (2 Sam 24), and a nation can be punished with poor leaders because the hearts of the people are evil (2 Kgs 17:1–23). In the same way, a nation can be blessed with good leadership because the people honor God (Prov 8:14–16; 2 Chr 7:14). We can honor the structure of leadership that God has ordained (Exod 18:21; Deut 17:14–20), and we can do this even if we do not agree with all the decisions those in authority are making; that's just all the more reason to pray for them.

ENDNOTES

1. Gary T. Meadors, "The Bible and Prayer," in *Giving Ourselves to Prayer: An Acts 6:4 Primer for Ministry*, comp. Dan R. Crawford (Terre Haute, IN: Prayer Shop Publishing), 10.

2. Adaptation of list compiled by AllAboutGOD.com, cited in "Why Pray?" National Day of Prayer Task Force, http://www.nationaldayofprayer.org (accessed October 6, 2010).

3. John Chrysostom, quoted in R. Kent Hughes, *James: Faith That Works* (Wheaton, IL: Crossway Books, 1991), 263.

4. The *Parade* Spirituality Poll, conducted by Insight Express, May 8–12, 2008, cited in Christine Wicker, "How Spiritual Are We?" October 4, 2009, http://www.parade.com/news/2009/10/04-how-spiritual-are-we.html (accessed October 6, 2010.

5. Federal Bureau of Investigation, Uniform Crime Reports, *Crime in the United States*, cited in Bureau of Justice Statistics, "Summary Findings," http://bjs.ojp.usdoj.gov/index.cfm?ty=tp&tid=3 (accessed October 6, 2010).

6. Jennifer Harper, "Study: Americans Pray Just to Get Through the Day," *Washington Times*, December 5, 2008, http://www.washingtontimes.com/news/2008/dec/05/study-americans-pray-just-to-get-through-the-day/.

7. National Day of Prayer Task Force, 2009 Media Kit, "Answer to Prayer," May 7, 2009.

8. Lawrence Jones, "Thousands Pray for Spiritual Revival at TheCall California," *Christian Post*, November 3, 2008, http://www.christianpost.com/article/20081103/thousands-pray-for-spiritual-revival-at-thecall-california/ (accessed October 7, 2010).

9. Adrienne S. Gaines, "National Day of Prayer May Be Largest-Ever," *Charisma News Online*, May 5, 2010, http://www.charismamag.com/index.php/news/28222-national-day-of-prayer-may-be-largest-ever.

10. Journals of America's National Prayer Committee, http://www.nationalprayer.org.

11. The National Day of Prayer Task Force, http://www.NationalDayofPrayer.org.

12. Heritage Builders Association, http://www.heritagebuilders.com.

13. Lifeway Research survey conducted April–May 2007, cited in Cathy Lynn Grossman, "Young Adults Aren't Sticking with Church," *USA Today*, August 6, 2007.

14. The Barna Group Ltd, "Twentysomethings Struggle to Find Their Place in Christian Churches," September 24, 2003, http://www.barna.org/barna-update/article/5-barna-update/127-twentysomethings-struggle-to-find-their-place-in-christian-churches?q=twentysomethings.

15. Frank D. Fincham, et al., "Spiritual Behaviors and Relationship Satisfaction: A Critical Analysis of the Role of Prayer," *Journal of Social and Clinical Psychology* 27, no. 4 (2008): 362–88.

16. M.G. Dudley and F.A. Kosinski, "Religiosity and Marital Satisfaction: A Research Note," *Review of Religious Research* 32 (1990): 78–86, cited in Fincham et al., "Spiritual Behaviors."

17. Heritage Builders Association, http://www.heritagebuilders.com.

CHAPTER TWO

THE BASELINE

JOHN BORNSCHEIN

The action of prayer is healthy for a home and a community. We know that God does hear these prayers, which is where the real power resides. You would not be reading this book unless you had some inkling that there is a Creator who you are accountable to and are seeking to understand more about His nature and how to dialogue with Him. This is the baseline that you must recognize before you make any further efforts to unravel the mysteries of prayer.

There is no basis for understanding prayer without first proclaiming that without a doubt, there is a God in heaven who created you and desires fellowship with you. As Anthony DeStefano states so well in his book, *Ten Prayers God Always Says Yes To,*

> There isn't much room for compromise here. Either we're alone in the world or we're not. Either we came about by chance or we were created for a reason. Either death is the end or it's the beginning. Either our situation is ultimately hopeless or it's ultimately blissful. There really can't be two more different or diametrically opposed worldviews. So how can we come to grips with this most profound question? Some of the greatest geniuses the world has ever

known—Aristotle, Plato, Augustine, Aquinas, Spinoza, Pascal, Descartes and Kant, to name a few—have made the case that there is a God, and that He is a real, living being. In the case of faith, it's easy to overlook the most fundamental point of all, namely, that God is not an argument; he is not a syllogism; He is not even a concept. God is a living being. He has the ability to know things, to desire things, to create things, and to love things. He is fully aware and involved. He is alive.[1]

Theology is our understanding of God. The term literally means "*logos* about *Theos*," or, a "word about God." The Christian faith is built on the foundation of trust in Almighty God who has revealed Himself to humanity. God the Father is the one who created the universe and sustains it, all while desiring a relationship with each one of us. "Almighty" means that God is sovereign over His creation. With wisdom and love, and in power and control, God presides over all things. His sovereignty is a source of comfort and truth for believers; we know that nothing happens without His knowledge and permission.

The words "Creator of heaven and earth" reflect our belief that all things were created by an orderly, wise God. Life has meaning and purpose. Humans bear God's image and likeness; therefore, all of life is to be respected, and creation should be valued. The complexity and design of the world around us lead us to the conclusion that there must be a grand designer or Creator. Empirical evidence found in life, chemistry, astrobiology, and especially physics suggests purpose, design, order, and meaning. Psalm 19:1 tells us that the created world points to the God who was its infinite originating source: "The heavens declare (or "bear witness to") the glory of God, and the firmament (or "expanse") shows His handiwork" (NIV).

What separates God from the rest of the spiritual or unseen entities, or even that which is in the physical world, is the fact that He is the *only* source of creation and life. There is no tangible evidence that suggests otherwise. God, Yahweh, the Alpha and the Omega, the only God by many names created the vast expanse of the universe and all that is within it, along with all dimensions, space, and time and the beings that inhabit them. And He created all of this from absolutely nothing. In fact, the human body is one of the most complex machines ever created. The bacterial flagellum is only between one and two microns in size, and yet it is one of most efficient rotary motors on the planet.

One cannot look at the universe and not see intelligent design. Human beings have created nothing. We have manipulated and shaped elements and worked within the confines of natural laws, but we have never created something from nothing. Even the theory of evolution is based on the "change in the inherited traits of a population of organisms from one generation to the next." It is the theory of natural selection over a large span of time. Regardless of the amount of time that is required for evolution to take place, the theory self-destructs when origin is examined. There is no beginning to the process that has a viable source without a Creator. Thus, we are right back to confronting the fact that an intelligent designer is at work, an engineer of a very complex system. R.C. Sproul writes that "men are never duly touched and impressed with a conviction of their insignificance, until they have contrasted themselves with the majesty of God."[2]

IMAGE OF GOD

If indeed there is a God, are we created in His likeness? The answer to this question is critical for establishing a baseline when discussing the principles of prayer and the origin of its power. According to Dr. Michael Behe, biophysics professor at Lehigh University, one could argue that the human body is more complex than the earth and its entire ecological system. However, is this vessel and its complexity what God was referring to when He stated in Genesis 1:26, "Let us make man in our image, after our likeness"?

Genesis 1:27 observes, "So God created mankind in his own image, in the image of God he created them; male and female he created them." Is the image of God the vessel of the human body, or is it something more? This is where we must begin in order to unravel the interpretation of this passage. Many scholars and theologians have attempted to answer the question, "What is the image of God?"

- Thomas Aquinas identified the image of God as "the human ability to think and reason, to use language and art, far surpassing the abilities of any animals."[3]
- Leonard Verduin stated that the image of God "consists in our dominion over animals and plants, which continues despite our sinfulness."[4]
- G.W. Bromiley notes that "A 'widely accepted interpretation' is that the 'image' is our ability to make moral decisions, which involve self-awareness and social awareness."[5]
- According to Emil Brunner, the image is "our ability to have a relationship with God, reflected in the tendency of all societies to have forms of worship."[6]

Many theologians believe there are three common elements within the concept of *imago Dei* (the "image of God"):

1. **Substantive:** The *substantive* element refers to the idea that humans were formed in the likeness of God in both characteristics and physical form. Many believe that God crafted our very design from His own makeup. According to this theory, God inhabits a body, and He used this perfect, flawless vessel as a blueprint for the human structure. In addition, we are formed in His likeness by our characteristics—our free will. We are not programmed by instinct, design, or function. We can execute decisions based on our thoughts. Martin Luther

suggested that humanity possessed the character of holiness—morality and love for God.

2. **Relational:** The *relational* element is based on the theology that we had a relationship with God before the fall of humanity, and to retain the image of God, we must have the Holy Spirit dwelling within us through a relationship with Christ. It is this gift that separates us from other complex living creatures. We are not organic machines. Rather, we are living souls that have a destination in the spiritual realm. We are symbiotic creations, evidenced by the fact that our living, breathing, physical body is controlled by a living soul.

3. **Functional:** The *functional* element focuses more on the second part of Genesis 1:26, which states, "Let them rule over the fish of the sea and the birds of the air, over the livestock, over all the earth, and over all the creatures that move along the ground." This theory suggests that the authority over creation is the image of God. God has authority over all creation, but He has granted this authority to humankind over the earth. Thus, all creation on earth is subject to the rule of humankind, just as the universe is subject to God.

Now we must examine God's word to pull the pieces together in our understanding of the image of God. Consider Psalm 139:14–16: "I praise you because I am fearfully and wonderfully made; your works are wonderful, I know that full well. My frame was not hidden from you when I was made in the secret place, when I was woven together in the depths of the earth. Your eyes saw my unformed body; all the days ordained for me were written in your book before one of them came to be." God tells the prophet Jeremiah something similar in Jeremiah 1:5—"Before I formed you in the womb I knew you, before you were born I set you apart." In both of these verses, we see a common thread: God knew the person before He made the body.

In the book of James, one of my favorite writings, we read two passages that build on this theme. James 3:9 states, "With the tongue we praise our Lord and Father, and with it we curse human beings, *who have been made in God's likeness*" (emphasis added). Later, James writes, "What is your life? *You are a mist that appears for a little while and then vanishes*" (Jas 4:14, emphasis added).

Do these verses contradict each other? If we are made in God's likeness, why does He use such blunt and even harsh words to describe the frailty of humanity? In chapter three, James is reprimanding us for "cursing" those who have been formed in God's likeness; yet only a few verses later, in chapter four, he tells us that we are nothing more than a mist—here today, gone tomorrow. Already, there is a distinction between the body and the soul.

Three verses from Genesis also stress that the body is limited— nothing more than flesh and bone, a vessel formed from the earth:

1. When God formed Eve, Adam said, "This is now bone of my bones, and flesh of my flesh; she shall be called 'woman' for she was taken out of man" (Gen 2:23).

2. In Genesis 3:19, God said to Adam, "By the sweat of your brow you will eat your food until you return to the ground, since from it you were taken; for dust you are and to dust you will return."

3. In Genesis 6:3, the Lord says, "My Spirit will not contend with man forever, for he is mortal; his days will be a hundred and twenty years."

These images of temporary flesh and bone are not the descriptions one would expect from the Designer, especially when the issue of a self-portrait is in question. Furthermore, throughout Scripture, we read of the torture and brutality suffered by those who called themselves Christians. Consider this passage from Hebrews: "There were others who were tortured, refusing to be released .... Some faced jeers and flogging, and even chains and imprisonment. They were put to death by stoning; they were sawed in two; they were killed by the sword. They went about in sheepskins and goatskins, destitute, persecuted and mistreated" (Heb 11:35–38).

If these Christians' bodies were the images of God, why were they so willing to sacrifice them to persecution, torture, and death? God's people treated holy objects like the ark of the covenant, the staff of Aaron, and the bronze snake post with great care and reverence. If Christ's followers were also regarded as holy temples of God's Spirit, wouldn't they treat their bodies with reverence as well?

Hebrews goes on to say that the sacrifice of these believers was motivated by their pure love of God. It seems that if the human body is made in the image and likeness of God, He would want us to treat His image with the utmost care and respect, regardless of our love for Him. Yet consider the motivation and sacrifice of God's own Son: "Since the children have flesh and blood, [Jesus] too shared in their humanity so that by his death he might break the power of him who holds the power of death—that is, the devil—and free those who all their lives were held in slavery by their fear of death" (Heb 2:14–16).

Christ was made a little lower than the angels when He took on human form to suffer and die as the ultimate sacrifice for sin. As Hebrews 2:6–7 states, "What is mankind that you are mindful of them, a son of man that you care for him? You made them a little lower than the angels; you crowned them with glory and honor." A parallel passage, Psalm 8:5, likewise says, "You have made them a little lower than the angels and crowned them with glory and honor."

Christ did not elevate His stature when He took on a human body; rather, the incarnation was a descent that made Him even lower than the angels. If He came to earth and lived as a perfect man in the image of God, would it not have been the other way around? Would not

He, in the flesh, have been exalted above His creation? Yet in God's redemptive plan, Jesus "made himself nothing by taking the very nature of a servant" (Phil 2:7). In the ultimate paradox, God, who created humanity in His own image, sent His Son to earth in "human likeness" (Phil 2:7), and this divine man "*humbled* himself by becoming obedient to death—even death on a cross" (Phil 2:8).

Hebrews 1:3–4 reveals the victory that flowed from such an amazing sacrifice: "After he had provided purification for sins, he sat down at the right hand of the Majesty in heaven. So he became as much superior to the angels as the name he has inherited is superior to theirs." Christ, who took on human flesh and placed Himself below the heavenly beings He had created, was exalted in the end, raised once more above the angels in honor and glory. Understanding the significance of the incarnation of Christ and God's redemptive purpose in creation is essential to understanding the image of God.

UNDERSTANDING REDEMPTION

Over and over in Scripture, we see a clear distinction between flesh and blood and the soul. The person (or soul) who inhabits a human body is known and loved by God. It is that person Christ died for. The body is formed, lives for up to 120 years, and then dies—a mere mist in the scope of eternity. It is the soul that God grants eternal life through Christ's sacrifice. The Apostle Paul wrote, "For we live by faith, not by sight. We are confident, I say, and would prefer to be away from the body and at home with the Lord. So we make it our goal to please him, whether we are at home in the body or away from it. For we must all appear before the judgment seat of Christ, that each of us may receive what is due us for the things done while in the body, whether good or bad" (2 Cor 5:7–10).

Clearly, the body is a vessel that we as persons inhabit. It is an earthly biomachine for our soul. If the legs work, we should use them to carry the message of God's love throughout the world. If the arms work, we should use them to minister to those in need. If the tongue works, we should use it to speak truth of the gospel and praise our Father in heaven. The body is not our final form. It is a means to an end—a temporary and necessary tool for doing the work of God in the physical world. Yet we must still answer this question: is the body designed in the image of God?

One could make the case that the human body and the soul that dwells within it are both shaped in the likeness of God. Our physical and spiritual traits are the aspects that separate us from all of creation. The human body is so complex that we have not yet begun to fully explore its depths. That complexity is symbolic of the very nature of God.

In Habakkuk 1:5, God declared, "Look at the nations and watch—and be utterly amazed. For I am going to do something in your days that you would not believe, even if you were told." This declaration foreshadowed the outpouring of God's power in the human soul through the Holy Spirit. Humanity reflects the true image of God when the soul is coupled with God's Spirit. The image of God is the personhood of the individual, who has been granted sonship by faith in Christ (Gal 3:26). It is the one who cries "Abba, Father."

The sons and daughters of the Most High, whose names are written in the Book of Life, are the ones who are truly made in the image of God. The body we have been given on this earth is a tribute to His creativity, a gift during our time here. Our ability to choose—to make either good and bad decisions—is a freedom we have been granted, but we reflect the image and likeness of God when we love holiness and morality. The transformed soul makes decisions and directs the body to follow a course that honors the Lord.

Romans 12:2 reminds those who bear God's image, "Do not conform to the pattern of this world, but be transformed by the renewing of your mind. Then you will be able to test and approve what God's will is—his good, pleasing and perfect will." Both the decisions of our minds and the actions of our bodies are subject to souls that are transformed into the likeness of Christ. This is expressed in 2 Corinthians 3:18: "And we, who with unveiled faces contemplate the Lord's glory, are being transformed into his image with ever-increasing glory, which comes from the Lord, who is the Spirit."

God breathed the Holy Spirit and all of His characteristics (Gal 5:16–26) into Adam and Eve when He created them. But the indwelling Spirit was lost when Adam and Eve disobeyed. The Scriptures tell us that "Then the Lord God formed a man from the dust of the ground and breathed into his nostrils the breath of life, and the man became a living being" (Gen 2:7). God did not breathe into the nostrils of all the living creatures, so what was the difference? Life was all around Adam, so what was the "breath of life" God instilled in man? It was the Spirit of God. He was in Adam and Eve at the beginning, but He departed when they chose evil and allowed sin to corrupt the perfection that was required for the Spirit of God to dwell within them.

It took another five thousand years before the sacrifice of Jesus Christ offered a way for humankind to be filled with His Spirit once again. The Spirit, who had not dwelt in the human heart since the fall, was poured out after the resurrection when Jesus breathed on His disciples and said, "Peace be with you! As the Father has sent me, I am sending you. … Receive the Holy Spirit" (John 20:21–22).

We must not forget that Jesus is the living Word of God, and He was "with God in the beginning" (John 1:1–2). This is why God said at creation, "Let us make mankind in *our image*" (Gen 1:26, emphasis added). Just as He gave the breath of life to Adam, God offers the breath of life to restore His image in those who have accepted the blood sacrifice of Jesus on their behalf. This acceptance of the blood reflects the Israelites' act of covering their doorposts in Egypt with the blood of sacrificial lambs to signify that they belonged to God (Exod 12:21–28; 1 Cor 5:7). Our bodies are now temples of the Holy Spirit (1 Cor 6:19; Eph 1:13–14)—as God initially designed us and always intended they should be. This is the image of God. Through Christ, we can attain that which was lost and be the light in a dark world.

ENDNOTES

1. Anthony DeStefano, *Ten Prayers God Always Says Yes To* (New York: Doubleday, 2007), 10–11.

2. R.C. Sproul, *The Holiness of God* (Wheaton, IL: Tyndale, 1985), 72.

3. Thomas Aquinas, "Man to the Image of God," cited in Millard J. Erickson, ed., *Readings in Christian Theology,* vol. 2, *Man's Need and God's Gift* (Grand Rapids: Baker Publishing Group, 1976), 37–43; Grace Communion International, "Humans in the Image of God," http://www.gci.org/humans/image (accessed October 7, 2010).

4. Leonard Verduin, "A Dominion-Haver," cited in Erickson, *Readings in Christian Theology,* 55–74; Grace Communion, "Humans in the Image of God."

5. G.W. Bromiley, "Image of God," cited in G.W. Bromiley, ed., *International Standard Bible Encyclopedia,* vol. 2 (Grand Rapids: Eerdmans, 1988), 804; Grace Communion, "Humans in the Image of God."

6. Emil Brunner, "Man and Creation," cited in Erickson, *Readings in Christian Theology,* 45–54; Grace Communion, "Humans in the Image of God."

CHAPTER THREE

ENLISTING: UNDERSTANDING PRAYER

JOHN BORNSCHEIN

To understand prayer is to conceptualize something that is far greater than human comprehension. Think for a moment about the universe, which contains more than one hundred billion galaxies, with more than one hundred billion stars per galaxy.[1] How can one explain that the God who created and holds in His hands such a vast universe (Job 37–39) can pause from all the demands for His attention to listen to, contemplate, and even act upon the petitions of human beings? Actually, it is not a matter of asking *how* God can pause to hear us pray, but *why*? Why would such a powerful and limitless entity, a force far greater than human words could ever describe, give ear to the thoughts and utterings of finite creatures—specks in such a grand and complex system? That is an exciting mystery in and of itself, and one that we will explore in this chapter.

But before we examine the strands of prayer that are woven throughout the tapestry of life, we must begin with a firm understanding that a satisfying prayer journey is only obtained in our desire for relationship with God.

The Creator has many names—Elohim, El Shaddai, Adonai, Yahweh, Theos, the Alpha and Omega. But according to the Bible, God is approachable and accessible through only one source: Jesus (or *Yeshua* in Hebrew). If you have not accepted the blood of Christ as the atonement for your sins, you cannot experience the fullness of relationship with God the Father through prayer. But the moment you receive God's gift of salvation, you are no longer a simple human. Rather, you become a child of the living God. This amazing transformation is described in the book of John: "Yet to all who did receive him [Jesus], to those who believed in his name, he gave the right to become children of God" (John 1:12). Like a caterpillar in a cocoon that passes through metamorphosis and becomes a butterfly, so you, too, through new birth in Christ, transform from the dust of the earth, from the old nature, into a new creation—that which is eternal (2 Cor 5:17–21; Rev 21). It is our identity in Christ that makes the dialogue of prayer possible.

DEFINING PRAYER

Jennifer Kennedy Dean states, "Prayer is an interchange of love between the Father and His child. That desire you feel to pray is His love drawing you to delight in Him. You only need to respond."[2] For true Christians, prayer (*proseuche* in Greek) is "communion with God." It is the medium of divine revelation. Through prayer, we actually experience relationship with God. The quality of our prayer life then determines the quality of our relationship with God.

Prayer is talking with God and listening to Him, and it is enjoying the presence of God. In his book, *Prayer on Fire*, Fred Hartley describes prayer as, "What we do. It is our initiative to meet God, whether we are asking for favors, singing in celebration, or crying out in distress. Regardless of what shape or size in comes in, prayer is our effort to engage God."[3] Prayer can take many forms, including worship, confession, thanksgiving, praise, petition (asking for what we need and desire), waiting (silent listening and sensing of God), and warfare (command).[4] As believers, we can pray in the Spirit—even in language that may be unknown to us but is fully known to God (1 Cor 14:2, 27–28).

Our goal through prayer must be to know God better, to experience the fullness of relationship with Him. Through prayer, we honor Him. We give something back to the Almighty, something He desires greatly. God reveals Himself to us in the "prayer closet"—a quiet place where we cannot be distracted in our time with Him.

If you do not desire to understand the deep things of God, if you do not desire to give praise to the Father, then the rest of this book will be of no use to you. Your mindset from this point on must be that you will no longer accept mediocrity in your life but will desire more in your relationship with God. You must be ready to break out of your ritualistic or traditional prayer practices, in which you may consider God as nothing more than a glorified genie in a bottle.

ABOVE ACTION

For years, I struggled with one-way dialogue in my prayer life. This was due to a narrow perspective of faith derived from works. In my mind, I lived by my religious to-do list, complete with check boxes: go to church on Sunday, go to church on Wednesday, read the Scriptures once a year (with a morning or bedtime routine of following outlined chapters), go to men's groups, tithe every Sunday. Oh, and be sure to pray before every meal and at the close of the day. These disciplines, though healthy, were practices that demonstrated my commitment to the Christian walk. But they were my works, not expressions of love for my God and King.

I have been blessed to serve in ministry for more than 20 years. During that time, I noticed a common practice among the men in our church: they were often motivated to express their faith by *doing* something. As long as they were engaged in some activity, they were passionate about their faith. But their fire would begin to fade when conversations about God focused solely on emotional expressions of love for Him. It was quickly rekindled when a task needed to be done, especially if the project involved a group of men working with their hands to accomplish something in the community. Why did the fire return when they were engaged in a project? It was tangible; the objective was clear, and the goal was attainable. Rather than simply talking about some abstract inner change, they were able to demonstrate the change in a practical and concrete way, doing something they considered to be "kingdom work."

There is nothing wrong with men or women expressing their faith and love for the Lord through works. After all, we were "created in Christ Jesus to do good works, which God prepared in advance for us to do" (Eph 2:10). But prayer is often lumped into the category of intangibles and, as such, it receives little emphasis.

In the past, it was easy for me to get caught up in tasks because I felt that viable, daily disciplines pleased God. These things came quite naturally to me as a man. Prayer, however, was nothing more than talking into the air for a set period of time—but at least I was able to check that task off my to-do list at the end of the day. Another accomplishment recorded in the books!

It is this focus on works that is the foundation of all religion. Yet throughout Scripture, we find that God desires more than religion; He wants relationship. Jesus calls out to each of us, "Here I am! I stand at the door and knock. If anyone hears my voice and opens the door, I will come in and eat with him, and he with me" (Rev 3:20).

My prayer journey took another step when I began to understand that there was a living God on the other end of the conversation. My words were, in fact, rising above the ceiling and reaching heaven. But I still did not fully grasp what prayer was intended to do. I am ashamed to say that it wasn't until recently that I finally began to comprehend the idea that praying is not about what God can do for me; it is about offering myself to Him, surrendering my own agenda, and seeking His glory instead. If we fail to cry out to Him, to praise Him, the rocks *will* (Luke 19:40). I don't know about you, but I don't want rocks taking my place worshiping the Creator of the universe, or fulfilling the purpose He intended for me.

BUILDING A RELATIONSHIP

God desires relationship, but for many years I was preoccupied with works. Not only that, I was preoccupied with self. When I prayed, it was a preconceived line of thought followed by a list of needs, and I was often impatient for results. In my mind, God needed to provide fast results, and if one prayer was not sufficient, I took measures into my own hands. Hey, at least I gave God a chance to perform, and then I did what any good Christian should do, right? But I was still missing the point.

The Apostle Paul tells us in Philippians 3:10,

> [For my determined purpose is] that I may know Him [that I may progressively become more deeply and intimately acquainted with Him, perceiving and recognizing and understanding the wonders of His Person more strongly and more clearly], and that I may in that same way come to know the power outflowing from His resurrection [which it exerts over believers], and that I may so share His sufferings as to be continually transformed [in spirit into His likeness even] to His death. (AMP)

And in Ephesians 1:17, he wrote, "I keep asking that the God of our Lord Jesus Christ, the glorious Father, may give you the Spirit of wisdom and revelation, so that you may know him better." Paul got it. And he wasn't alone. Enoch, the great-grandfather of Noah, had such a deep relationship with God that one day God just took him to heaven (Gen 5:22–23). Later, Elijah, who lived every day in wholehearted devotion to the Father, was escorted to heaven in a chariot of fire. That must have been an incredible sight.

Throughout time, God has opened Himself up to men and women to initiate friendship. Friends with the Almighty—what a concept! In *Ten Prayers God Always Says Yes To*, DeStefano states,

The fact is that we have a God who loves to communicate. And the reason is that communication is the starting point for any relationship. Everyone has heard it said that God wants to be able to have a relationship with us. There is no truer point in all theology. Indeed, the thrust of God's communication with mankind over the course of history has always been relational and not conceptual. That's why he actually prefers it when we come to have faith in him through prayer, instead of through logical arguments alone. God doesn't just want to satisfy a curiosity we have, He wants to enter into a friendship with us.[5]

God called King David, arguably one of the greatest kings who ever reigned on the earth, a man after His own heart. David poured out his love, respect, and humility before God throughout the Psalms. In Psalm 63:1, David expressed his thirst for the living God: "You, God, you are my God, earnestly I seek you; I thirst for you, my whole being longs for you, in a dry and weary land where there is no water." God designed us to thirst for Him. Many try to quench this thirst by pursuing physical desires, but this is a hopeless quest with no resolution. As Jesus said, "Everyone who drinks [natural] water will be thirsty again, but whoever drinks the water I give them will never thirst. Indeed, the water I give them will become in them a spring of water welling up to eternal life" (John 4:13–14).

If you knew that ours was the last generation before the coming of Christ, how would you live? When you stand before the throne of God, will you know Him intimately as your friend, or will you be a stranger? Are you going through the routine of your Christian walk without experiencing friendship with Elohim? Through Spirit-led prayer, your eyes will be opened, and you will have an indescribable relationship with God that is rich and fulfilling.

In *Experiencing Prayer with Jesus,* Dr. Henry Blackaby writes, "How deep is your relationship with the Lord as you pray? Do you pour your heart out to Him with complete confidence and trust in His help, because you've come to know and experience His love? It takes time, like any relationship. The more time you spend with Him, the more you'll come to understand His ways, His heart, and His will as you pray."[6] It is my hope that when you have completed this study, you will never view prayer the same way again, and you will experience true intimacy with the Almighty each time you fall to your knees, clasp your hands, and speak before the throne of the Most High.

THE BASICS OF PRAYER

At the National Day of Prayer Task Force, we developed a simple PRAY acrostic to help people remember the basic elements of prayer:[7]

> **P**raise
>
> **R**epent
>
> **A**sk
>
> **Y**ield

Before we request anything of the Father, we worship Him with heartfelt words of praise. (If you need help in this area, select a psalm from the Bible and read it to the Lord.) In her book, *Certain Peace in Uncertain Times*, Shirley Dobson writes, "He invites us into conversation with Him because it brings Him pleasure. That's sometimes a little hard to believe, isn't it? The holy and perfect and all-powerful ruler of the universe enjoys our prayers of praise? But the proof is in the Scripture: 'The prayer of the upright is His delight' (Prov 15:8 NKJV). God actually delights in and pursues our worship."[8] In Matthew 6:6–13, Christ provides a model of prayer for His followers:

> When you pray, go into your room, close the door and pray to your Father, who is unseen. ... And when you pray, do not keep on babbling like pagans, for they think they will be heard because of their many words. Do not

be like them, for your Father knows what you need before you ask him.

This, then, is how you should pray: "Our Father in heaven, hallowed be your name, your kingdom come, your will be done, on earth as it is in heaven. Give us today our daily bread. And forgive us our debts, as we also have forgiven our debtors. And lead us not into temptation, but deliver us from the evil one."

With this very powerful prayer, Jesus made sure we would cover the essential points in our conversation with the King. We *praise* Him, for He alone is worthy to be praised. We *repent* of sin, asking forgiveness so that nothing will hinder us from receiving the blessing of response. We then *ask* for those things we need and *yield* to His will, for He alone knows how best to respond to our petitions.

As we grow in our relationship with the Father, we will understand more clearly how to pray according to His will. Read again these words of James: "When you ask, you do not receive, because you ask with wrong motives, that you may spend what you get on your pleasures" (Jas 4:3). When we are focused on our own desires, we aren't praying with God's will in mind. James points out that one reason God doesn't answer our prayers is that our motives are self-centered and wrong. But when we *yield* our desires to Him, we find true contentment, receiving with grateful hearts whatever God provides. As the Apostle Paul states in 1 Timothy 6:8: "If we have food and clothing, we will be content with that."

Although Scripture tells us that we have whatever we ask in Jesus' name (John 16:23), God may say no to our requests and even allow us to go through suffering. The Apostle Paul was well acquainted with suffering. In 2 Timothy, He offers these words to encourage us in the midst of our sorrow: "Join with me in suffering, like a good soldier of Christ Jesus" (2 Tim 2:3) and "Keep your head in all situations, endure hardship" (2 Tim 4:5). Peter also encouraged those who were suffering, writing, "Do not be surprised at the fiery ordeal that has come on you to test you. … But rejoice inasmuch as you participate in the sufferings of Christ, so that you may be overjoyed when his glory is revealed" (1 Pet 4:12–13).

ETERNAL

E.M. Bounds dedicated countless years of his life to exploring the depth of prayer. In his writings on prayer, he states the following:

> The most important lesson we can learn is how to pray. Indeed, we must pray so that our prayers take hold of God. The man who has done the most and the best praying is the most immortal, because prayers do not die. Perhaps the lips that uttered them are closed in death, or the heart that felt them may have ceased to beat, but the prayers live before God, and God's heart is set on them. Prayers outlive the lives of those who uttered them … [they] outlive a generation, outlive an age, outlive a world.[9]

Bounds makes a life-changing point: our bodies will age and die, but the prayers that leave our tongues are a blessing to the Father for all eternity.

Chapters 5 and 8 of Revelation describe the prayers of saints as golden bowls full of incense rising to God as a fragrant sacrifice. Some versions say that the incense is a sweet aroma to His nostrils. The text doesn't specify the age of the prayers, only that they were brought carefully into the throne room by the angels. We cannot see our prayers rising like incense to heaven or grasp their enduring quality, but our prayers are eternal. As Paul wrote, "So we fix our eyes not on what is seen, but on what is unseen, since what is seen is temporary, but what is unseen is eternal" (2 Cor 4:18).

THREE WISHES

How do you pray? I used to treat God as though He was supposed to grant me three wishes when I prayed. My prayers were filled with "Do this," "Do that," "I need this," "I need that." Believe me; it is easy to pray this way. But when we do, we act like spoiled children, demanding the benefit of the relationship's power but failing to build the relationship. We perform our Christian duties, and then we list the things we need from God.

Are you throwing a short prayer His way before you eat, while stuck in traffic, or when you are looking for the best parking spot? Or are you actively pursuing a relationship with the Father through prayer? If you are a parent, what would you rather hear from the child you love? "Thanks for the food, you're neat, let's eat," or "I miss you. I really look forward to our time together. I long to be with you. I know you have everything worked out already, but I am worried about some things today. I need your help; I really blew it today. You told me what to do, but I still messed up. I will do better tomorrow. But I really need you to be with me, because I am weak. All I really want to do is make you happy. I love you so much. I want to know you more each and every day. Help me and please forgive me."

What is the difference between these two prayers? The heart. The purpose, the intent, and the respect are transparent. Prayer is not a fitful, short-lived exercise. It is not a voice crying unheard and unheeded in the silence. It is a voice that reaches God's ear. And it lives as long as that ear is open to holy pleas, as long as His heart is alive to holy things—and we know it always is.

A HOUSE OF PRAYER

E.M. Bounds writes, "The life of the church is the highest life, and its office is to pray. When God's house on the earth is a house of prayer, then God's house in heaven is busy and powerful in its plans and movements. 'For mine house shall be called a house of prayer for all people' (Isa 56:7)."[10]

God shapes the world by prayer. The more praying there is in the world, the better the world will be, and the mightier the forces against evil everywhere. Prayer, in one phase of its operation, is a disinfectant and a preventive. Prayer is God's settled and singular condition to further His Son's kingdom on earth (Matt 6:10). Therefore, the believer who is the most highly skilled in prayer will do the most for God. Men and women are to pray for the advancement of God's cause. The one who knows how to wield the power of prayer is the strong one, the holy one in Christ's kingdom. He is one of God's heroes, saints, servants, and agents.

Jesus tells believers, "Ask, and it shall be given you; seek, and you shall find; knock, and it shall be opened unto you" (Matt 7:7 KJV). The strongest disciple in Christ's kingdom is the one who can knock the best. The secret of success in Christ's kingdom is the ability to pray.

ENDNOTES

1. Kenneth Brecher, "Galaxy," World Book Online Reference Center (2005), cited in World Book at NASA, s.v. "Galaxy," NASA, http://www.nasa.gov/worldbook/galaxy_worldbook.html (accessed October 9, 2010).

2. Jennifer Kennedy Dean, *Heart's Cry: Principles of Prayer* (Birmingham: New Hope Publishers, 2007), 18.

3. Fred A. Hartley, III, *Prayer on Fire: What Happens When the Holy Spirit Ignites Your Prayers* (Colorado Springs: NavPress, 2006), 16.

4. List compiled by All About God Ministries, http://www.AllAboutGod.com, cited on National Day of Prayer Task Force Web site, http://www.nationaldayofprayer.org.

5. Anthony DeStefano, *Ten Prayers God Always Says Yes To: Divine Answers to Life's Most Difficult Problems* (New York: Doubleday, 2007), 13.

6. Henry Blackaby and Norman Blackaby, *Experiencing Prayer with Jesus: The Power of His Presence and Example* (Sisters, OR: Multnomah), 28.

7. National Day of Prayer Task Force, "P.R.A.Y." copyright 1994, used by permission.

8. Shirley Dobson, Certain Peace in Uncertain Times: Embracing Prayer in an Anxious Age (Carol Stream, IL: Tyndale, 2008).

9. E.M. Bounds, E.M. Bounds on Prayer (New Kensington, PA: Whitaker House, 1997), 11, 19, 34–36, 42.

10. E.M. Bounds, *E.M. Bounds on Prayer*.

CHAPTER FOUR

BASIC TRAINING: THE FULLNESS OF PRAYER

JOHN BORNSCHEIN

At this point you should understand the basic premise of prayer: relationship with the Father. In prayer, we align our direction with God's will. If you have not done so already, you need to learn to balance your study of the Scriptures and your quiet time. God will reveal Himself to you through your diligent pursuit of Him. However, when you dedicate time to Him in prayer, it is there that He will unravel some of the mysteries of the gospel and give you wisdom to navigate and understand the deep things of His holy nature. This is where the relationship develops. It is an awesome experience when you dive into the waters of truth.

So, how do we begin to experience the fullness of prayer—the deeper understanding of its purpose? Throughout Scripture, we are reminded to petition the Father with our requests. In Matthew 18:19–20, Jesus told His disciples, "… if two of you on earth agree about anything they ask for, it will be done for them by my Father in heaven. For where two or more gather in my name, there am I with them." These verses provide the fundamentals of experiencing the fullness of prayer:

- "I will proclaim the LORD's decree. … *Ask me*, and I will make the nations your inheritance" (Psa 2:7–8, emphasis added).

- "*Ask me* of things to come concerning my sons, and concerning the work of my hands command ye me" (Isa 45:11 KJV, emphasis added).
- "*Call to me*, and I will answer you and tell you great and unsearchable things you do not know" (Jer 33:3, emphasis added).
- "You may *ask me for anything in my name*, and I will do it" (John 14:14, emphasis added).
- "You do not have *because you do not ask God*. When you ask, you do not receive, because you ask with wrong motives, that you may spend what you get on your pleasures" (Jas 4:2–3, emphasis added).

The common point in all these verses is this: we have to ask in order to receive. That is not too difficult to remember, and it might be how we spend the most of our prayer time. However, asking goes deeper than this. God wants to give to us and care for us (Matt 6:28–33; Luke 11:11–13). It is in His nature as our Father; after all, we are His children. We just need to remind ourselves that it is about relationship, not privilege. Our hearts are not in the right place if we simply call on the Lord for answers to prayer without desiring to know Him as our Father (Isa 29:13).

DEFYING TIME

Here is a thought that may rock your very foundation. In 1905, Albert Einstein first proposed his theory of special relativity, which relates to the speed of light in relation to "inertial objects," or objects at rest. Five years later, he introduced general relativity, which "demonstrates that time is [inextricably] linked … to matter and space, and thus the dimensions of time, space, and matter constitute … a continuum."[1]

According to the theory of special relativity, two people observing the same event in the same way could perceive the singular event occurring at two different times, depending upon their distance from the event in question. What accounts for this difference is the time it takes for light to travel through space. Since light travels at a finite and ever constant speed, an observer from a more distant point will perceive an event as occurring later in time; however, the event is "actually" occurring at the same instant in time. Thus, time is dependent on space.[2]

On September 10, 2008, the Large Hadron Collider (LHC), which is located in an underground tunnel on the Franco-Swiss border between the Jura Mountains and the Alps near Geneva, Switzerland, circulated its first particle beams. The LHC was built by the European Organization for Nuclear Research (CERN) at a cost of nearly five billion dollars. It is the world's largest and highest-energy particle accelerator, intended to collide opposing beams of protons with very high kinetic energy. Its main purpose is to explore the validity and limitations of the current theoretical picture for particle physics.[3] However, it may also be the means for unlocking the string theory, which suggests that there are 11 dimensions in the universe—not just four, as Einstein had theorized. The very concept predicts that an intelligent force could travel through space and time and be in a million places at once, conducting a million conversations without time ever passing.

There are several things to consider here. First, it is incredible how capable the human mind is. What an amazing design, courtesy of God Himself! The brain can process and store more than 25 thousand books worth of data[4]—more than the Library of Congress can store. But God will only allow people to learn and accomplish so much; we know this from the story of Babel, where men were building great and mighty things, including a tower to God (Gen 11). The LHC is really no different. However, it has enabled us to ask the questions, contemplate, and dwell on the idea that God, like the very concept of eternity, has no bounds. He is not limited to space and time. As the psalmist observed, "A thousand years in your sight are like a day that has just gone by, or like a watch in the night" (Psa 90:4). Peter echoed these words: "With the Lord a day is like a thousand years, and a thousand years are like a day" (2 Pet 3:8).

At a meeting of the Christian Leadership Alliance at Focus on the Family, physician and author Dr. Richard Swenson spoke on the subject of God in relation to space and time. He asked the audience, "Is it possible to pray today for something that affected yesterday? Space and time are no limits to God. If He knew you before He made you, He heard you before the words left your lips." Swenson wasn't encouraging the audience to pray for God to change the past; he was simply trying to get them to break out of their mental boxes and understand that the living God can pause and listen to our every word. He can think about our words and determine if and when He should act upon our request. He is able to do this for millions of people at the same time; He could spend a million years thinking about our prayers, and not one second would go by for humanity. Is that not a mind buster?

David seemed to understand that God was not bound by time and space when he wrote, "All the days ordained for me were written in your book before one of them came to be" (Psa 139:14–16). When you pray, your conversation with God has no bounds. It even breaks the limits of space and time. In the words of E.M. Bounds, "Prayer is the easiest and hardest of all things. It is the simplest and the most sublime, the weakest and the most powerful. Its results lie outside the range of human possibilities; they are limited only by the omnipotence of God."[5]

LIBERATING THE PASSION

Prayer is an act of submission. Remember, praying is not about us; it is about what we give back to Him, who first loved us. We may never see some of our prayers answered in our lifetime, but we must tarry with our Father. As Hosea the prophet said, "Let us press on to know the Lord" (Hos 6:3 NASB).

And prayer is simply an expression of faith. Prayer and a holy life are one and the same; they mutually act and react. Neither can survive alone, for the absence of one is the absence of the other. The deep things of God are learned only in prayer. Our whole being must be in our praying, just like John Knox when he declared, "Give me Scotland, or may I die." What passion Knox had for a piece of land!

Why do we often lack a passion for prayer? What holds us back? Our passion may be diminished because we are holding on to something that prevents us from communicating clearly with God. Or we may be harboring some sin we haven't confessed. Whatever may be at the root of our struggle with prayer, our Father knows exactly what is holding us back from experiencing the fullness of a relationship with Him. We need to confess it to the Lord so that nothing will interfere with our connection to Him (1 John 1:9).

The book of Hebrews encourages us to "throw off everything that hinders and the sin that so easily entangles. And let us run with perseverance the race marked out for us" (Heb 12:1). Instead of giving in to our weaknesses, sins, and failings, we must learn to pray "with all perseverance" (Eph 6:18 NKJV). Philip Henry said, "The best way to fight against sin [or any other struggle] is to fight it on our knees."

The Bible shows us repeatedly that one person can change the world through prayer:

- Elijah prayed for the rain to stop, and for over three years, it didn't rain (1 Kgs 17:1–7).
- Moses saved Israel from destruction by pleading with God (Num 14:13–19).
- Abraham's servant asked God to grant him success in his search for a wife for Isaac, and God led him to Rebekah (Gen 24:12–15). Isaac and Rebekah would give birth to Jacob, from whom the 12 tribes of Israel came.

God heard the prayers of these godly men, and He will hear our prayers, too. We have incredible power in prayer—far more than we can imagine.

ORIGIN OF THE POWER OF PRAYER

What power enables us to have a voice before God? In Genesis 6, God gave His covenant to Noah and spared his family from the devastating flood that came upon the earth because of sin. Noah was 10 generations removed from Adam (approximately 1,700 years). For 40 days and 40 nights, while the rains fell upon the earth, this covenant was preserved in a wooden ark made of cypress wood and covered in pitch.

Fast forward to the time of Moses, approximately 1,700 years after the flood. For 40 days and 40 nights (Exod 24:18), God gave His covenant to Moses and told Him to build a different ark. This ark was made of acacia wood, 3 ¾ feet long, 2 ¼ feet wide, and 2 ¼ feet tall, and covered in pure gold, both inside and out. It also featured cherubim facing each other, looking toward the cover. The lid of the ark was called the atonement cover, a very symbolic foreshadowing. Three times in Exodus 25, God told to Moses to put His testimony (or covenant) in the ark (25:10–22). Inside the ark was a "gold jar of manna, Aaron's staff that had budded, and the stone tablets of the covenant" (Heb 9:4).

The ark contained God's presence and power, and the Israelites were able to accomplish great things when they respected His presence and followed His commands. They were afraid to go to battle without the ark leading the way before them. With it, they knew no foe could prevail against them. Wherever the Israelites went, they witnessed the power of God in the ark. Here are just a few examples of this power:

- It stopped the flow of a mighty river (Josh 3).
- It brought down the walls of cities (Josh 6).
- It stopped the sun (Josh 10).
- It broke down idols and destroyed armies (1 Sam 5–6).

What was the source of the ark's power? The Holy Spirit (1 Kgs 8:27; Acts 7:44–45). This was the same Holy Spirit whom Christ said would come after His ascension (John 14:15–26; 16:5–15), the same Holy Spirit who inhabits those who have accepted the life-giving blood of Jesus. First Corinthians 6:19–20 says, "Do you not know that *your bodies are temples of the Holy Spirit*, who is in you, whom you have received from God? You are not your own; you were bought at a price. Therefore honor God with your bodies" (emphasis added; read also Eph 1:13–14). As believers in Christ, we are now temples of the Holy Spirit, whose power flows through us. What an incredible thought!

No wonder Jesus told His disciples, "If you have faith as small as a mustard seed, you can say to this mountain, 'Move from here to there,' and it will move. Nothing will be impossible for you" (Matt 17:20–21). But remember, this kind of spirit can come out only by prayer (Mark 9:29). If the very power that was able to stop the sun dwells in your body, what is stopping you from taking the sword that belongs to you? You are the ark of the covenant on two legs. Your body is now gold in the eyes of the Lord, and the atonement covering is the blood of Christ.

Acts 2 describes the flames that rested on the heads of the apostles as they gathered to pray before the Holy Spirit came upon them. Just as the burning bush that Moses encountered in the desert radiated God's presence, the flames at Pentecost were manifestations of God's Spirit. Now, the Holy Spirit is free to dwell in believers by the blood of Christ, and God will give the Holy Spirit to all who ask (Luke 11:13).

An amazing transition occurred from the law to grace. Under the law, people demonstrated their love for God by their actions. Hebrews 11 lists the men and women in the Old Testament who acted upon their love for the Lord. But in the New Testament, you see a significant transition. Rather than focusing on actions alone, Christ began holding people accountable for their thoughts and the desires of their hearts. For example, in the Sermon on the Mount, He told those who gathered, "You have heard that it was said, 'You shall not commit adultery.' But I tell you that anyone who looks at a woman lustfully has already committed adultery with her in his heart" (Matt 5:27–28).

Why would Christ raise the standard of holiness? Because God wants those who have a relationship with Him to think and act like He does. Sin is sin, regardless of whether it is an action or a thought. Christ wants us to put off the old practices of our sinful nature and draw closer to Him. He wants us to love holiness as He does. And He enables us to do this by the power of the Holy Spirit.

Galatians 5:22–23 tells us that "the fruit *of the Spirit* is love, joy, peace, forbearance, kindness, goodness, faithfulness, gentleness and self-control" (emphasis added). The Holy Spirit produces *His fruit* in us; it is not fruit we grow in our own power or effort.

Under the law, people performed to prove their love for God and to earn His favor; now, under grace, we perform because we are already loved and forgiven. Our actions flow from our love for Him because we know that He accepts and loves us in Christ. And we are filled with His love through the power of the Spirit.

KNOW THE ONE YOU'RE PRAYING TO

Robert Murray McCheyne, a 19th century Scottish preacher, wrote, "There is a constant tendency to omit adoration when I forget to whom I am speaking, when I rush heedlessly into the presence of Jehovah without thought of His awe-inspiring name and character. When I have little eyesight for His glory, and little admiration of His wonders, my heart has a native tendency to omit giving thanks, and yet it is especially commanded."[6] Even though Christ gave His life for us on the cross and calls us friends, and even His sons and daughters, we must remember that we are approaching a holy God who is receiving praise at this very moment from angels.

When Moses approached the burning bush, God said, "Do not come any closer. … Take off your sandals, for the place where you are standing is holy ground" (Exod 3:5). When we go before the most powerful, most holy, most high God, we dare not go disrespectfully. We are also reminded of this in Ecclesiastes 5:2: "Do not be hasty in word or impulsive in thought to bring up a matter in the presence of God. For God is in heaven and you are on the earth; therefore let your words be few" (NASB). I've found that Revelation 4:5–11 and Ezekiel 1:26–28 also serve as regular reminders of where we are when we pray as they provide a breathtaking illustration of God's throne and glory. Ezekiel describes his own response to God's glory:

> High above on the throne was a figure like that of a man. I saw that from what appeared to be his waist up he looked like glowing metal, as if full of fire, and that from there down he looked like fire; and brilliant light surrounded him. Like the appearance of a rainbow in the clouds on a rainy day, so was the radiance around him.
>
> This was the appearance of the likeness of the glory of the LORD. When I saw it, I fell facedown, and I heard the voice of one speaking." (Ezek 1:26–28)

When I read these passages, I cannot help but come into God's presence with praise. We must have our compasses aligned correctly so we know whom we are praying to and what He expects. We cannot determine our prayer walk by feelings alone.

Brian Toon, a distinguished former member of the National Prayer Committee, has told me many stories of his days flying in the U.S. Navy. He was an F-14 Tomcat pilot and later became an Air Boss. Brian says that when pilots fly at night, they must adapt to watching and trusting their instruments and gauges. At night, a pilot can make several critical errors if he operates by his senses. In fact, the body will adjust so much that a pilot could be flying upside down and feel right side up. As the pilot pulls on the stick, thinking he is climbing in altitude, he actually flies straight into the ground.

The same is true when it comes to our spiritual lives. The Apostle Paul said, "The person without the Spirit does not accept the things that come from the Spirit of God but considers them foolishness, and cannot understand them because they are discerned only through the Spirit" (1 Cor 2:14). If you think you understand spiritual things and know the one you're praying to, but you are not pursuing God's wisdom and direction through a balance of Scripture study and prayer, you may be off course. So stay focused and run the race to win the prize (1 Cor 9:24).

ENDNOTES

1. "Theory of Relativity: A Brief History," All About Science, http://www. allaboutscience.org/theory-of-relativity.htm (accessed October 10, 2010).

2. Wikipedia, s.v. "Special Relativity," http://en.wikipedia.org/wiki/Special_ relativity; http://en.wikipedia.org/wiki/Principle_of_relativity (accessed October 10, 2010).

3. Wikipedia, s.v. "Large Hadron Collider," http://en.wikipedia.org/wiki/Large_ Hadron_Collider (accessed October 10, 2010).

4. Craig Karges, *Ignite Your Intuition,* (Deerfield Beach, FL: Health Communications, 1999), 15.

5. E.M. Bounds, *E.M. Bounds on Prayer* (New Kensington, PA: Whitaker House, 1997).

6. Andrew Murray McCheyne, http://famousquotesandauthors.com.

CHAPTER FIVE

ADVANCED TRAINING: SUSTAINING A RELATIONSHIP

JOHN BORNSCHEIN

T hree aspects of prayer are essential to sustaining an ongoing relationship with the Father:

1. Pursue God's will from the moment you rise each morning, making it your sole mission to please Him.

2. Use your lips to praise God in worship and prayer.

3. Petition the Father regularly for the needs of others through intercessory prayer.

STARTING OUT THE DAY RIGHT

Martin Luther once said, "Work, work, from early until late. In fact, I have so much to do that I shall spend the first three hours in prayer." What a paradigm shift! Even now, as you read these words, you may be thinking about all the things that you need to accomplish. The tasks of the day can be overwhelming for many of us. It was no different for Martin Luther. But he knew he couldn't face the obstacles and challenges of the day without God's hand guiding him. Just being in the presence of the Lord for a moment of solitude at the beginning of each day can ease your burdens, renew your vision, and replenish the spiritual stores of wisdom you need to make decisions through the day.

When I first began praying every morning, I found it difficult to pray for even 10 minutes; now, I often find myself in prayer for hours. And I've since found that my day is more productive and my mind is better prepared when I commit my morning to prayer. The Psalms offer ample evidence that King David understood this essential practice as well:

- "In the morning, Lord, you hear my voice; in the morning I lay my requests before you and wait expectantly" (Psa 5:3).
- "I will sing of your strength, in the morning I will sing of your love; for you are my fortress, my refuge in times of trouble" (Psa 59:16).
- "O God, You are my God; Early will I seek You" (Psa 63:1 NKJV).
- "But I cry to you for help, Lord; in the morning my prayer comes before you" (Psa 88:13).

William Wilberforce also spoke of the importance of regular prayer, early and often: "Of all things, guard against neglecting God in the prayer closet. There is nothing more fatal to the life and power of religion. More solitude and earlier hours—pray three times a day, at least. How much better might I serve if I cultivated a closer communion with God!"[1]

If pleasing God is our only mission as we rise each morning, then pursuing Him in the morning shows respect and honor for the One who will direct our path throughout the day. If we start the day seeking God's will for our lives, then the rest will fall in line. We may encounter conflicts and difficulties throughout the day, but it will be much easier to maintain a godly perspective and make wise decisions if we have started our day with our eyes fixed on Jesus. When we open our hearts to God in this way, we won't be able to contain the outpouring of our affection and praise to Him.

USING YOUR LIPS

Scripture calls praise the "fruit" of our lips (Heb 13:15). With our lips, we glorify God, praise Him, and honor Him. The Psalms often describe audible praise as well. For example, Psalm 63:3–4 states, "Because your love is better than life, my lips will glorify you. I will praise you as long as I live." Similarly, Psalm 66:2 calls the people to "Sing out the honor of His name; make His praise glorious" (Psa 66:2 NKJV).

When David sang and danced before the Lord, his wife reprimanded him (2 Sam 6:12–23). But David was spot on; he didn't need to be reserved in expressing his love for God and the works of His hands. David was so close to the Almighty, he was unable to contain his passion.

If you pray in silence most of the time, I would encourage you to have a conversation aloud with God. Find a place where you can have some privacy—perhaps a hillside or a private room—and where you will be free to worship and pray without the fear of being seen or heard. You may be surprised to discover that verbalizing your prayers enables you to open up to God in a way you've never experienced. Later on, you may not be concerned about privacy, but for now, find a place where only you and the Father can converse without interruption. Then talk to Him, literally. Use the lips and the tongue He gave you. God wants to hear from you!

If you prefer praying in silence, He will hear those prayers as well. Silent prayer can be just as powerful and effective as audible prayer. The point I am making is this: if God has given you lips, *use them* for His kingdom.

And remember, praise starts with the heart; what proceeds from our lips is an expression of the soul. In Matthew 12:34, Jesus said, "For the mouth speaks what the heart is full of." We can go through the motions of praising God with our lips but our hearts are cold and distant from God, our worship is only empty words. The Lord rebuked His people for this attitude, saying, "These people come near to me with their mouth and honor me with their lips, but their hearts are far from me" (Isa 29:13).

INTERCESSORY PRAYER

Intercessory prayer is petitioning the Father for the needs of others. Intercession is mentioned more than 80 times in Scripture. The Hebrew word for "intercession" is *paga*, which means "to light upon." The Greek equivalent, *entygchano*, refers to conversation with a king that involves supplication and intercession on behalf of another person. The Greek word *paracletos*, referring to "one who pleads another's cause before a judge" is most closely linked to intercession in the New Testament.

If we are to model ourselves after Christ, we must be willing to give ourselves to prayer and fasting. The power of our relationship with God will come through concentrated devotion to others and their well-being. Hebrews 9:15 states that "Christ is the mediator of a new covenant" and is seeking those who will intercede for others—those willing to stand in the gap. In Genesis 18:22–23, we read that Abraham stood before the Lord to intercede for Sodom. But the Masoretic Text says that *the Lord stood before Abraham* and asked him to intercede. According to tradition, servants stood in the presence of kings—not the other way around—so English translations of this passage often show Abraham standing before the Lord. This translation may be culturally accurate, but it prevents us from seeing the intercessory heart of our God. He is the One who stands in the gap, petitioning for mercy on behalf of humankind, despite our sin. In a sense, God is petitioning Himself on our behalf. The ultimate example of this is Jesus, who stood before God as our Intercessor when He gave Himself for us on the cross.

God also stood in the gap to intercede for the Ninevites. He commanded Jonah to go to Nineveh and teach those lost men and women the truth so that they could be saved from God's judgment

(Jonah 1:1–2). He wanted Jonah to be selfless and intercede for those who did not deserve it. God's heart always seeks to intercede for us.

In the same way, we are to be imitators of the Divine Mediator. Ephesians 5:1–2 says, "Follow God's example, therefore, as dearly loved children and walk in the way of love, just as Christ loved us and gave himself up for us as a fragrant offering and sacrifice to God." As children of the living God, we must have God's heart—a heart of mercy and perseverance. We have been given the power of the Holy Spirit so that we can cry out to Him in intercession for others: "The Spirit you received does not make you slaves, so that you live in fear again; rather, the Spirit you received brought about your adoption to sonship. And by him we cry, 'Abba, Father'" (Rom 8:15). In Greek, Christ refers to the Father as "the sending me Father" that He might intercede on behalf of those who were doomed to perish.

Moses, Elijah, Samuel, and Nehemiah all interceded on behalf of Israel, and God heard them. One of the greatest examples of intercession took place when Moses stood before God on behalf of Israel. In Exodus 32:10, God said, "Leave me alone so that my anger may burn against them [the Israelites] and that I may destroy them." But Moses did not give up. And because God had a relationship with Moses, He allowed Moses to state the case on behalf of the people. In Exodus 32:14, we read that "the Lord relented and did not bring on his people the disaster he had threatened."

The account doesn't end there. Later, "Moses went back to the Lord and said, 'Oh, what a great sin these people have committed! They have made themselves gods of gold. But now, please forgive their sin—but if not, then blot me out of the book you have written'" (Exod 32:31–32). What a model of intercession! Moses was willing to lose his eternal inheritance on behalf of his people. He was willing to die for them, despite their transgressions.

King David referred to this event later in Psalm 106:23: "So [God] said he would destroy them—had not Moses, his chosen one, stood in the breach before him to keep his wrath from destroying them." Like the Israelites, we deserve to die for our sin. But just as Moses interceded for them, so has Christ interceded for us.

Over and over again, God Himself seeks those who are willing to put themselves on the line on behalf of others, those who are willing to walk through the fire if needed. Isaiah 59:16 states, "He [the Lord] saw that there was no one, he was appalled that there was no one to intervene." Similarly, Ezekiel 22:30 shows the Lord seeking an intercessor: "I looked for someone among them [the Israelites] who would build up the wall and stand before me in the gap on behalf of the land so I would not have to destroy it, but I found no one."

Intercessory prayer is more than simply praying a few words on behalf of someone and then moving on to other requests, never praying for that person or concern again. Intercession is pouring out our hearts for others, taking on the burden of those who are going through a trial.

PRACTICING PERSISTENCE

First Thessalonians 5:17 tells us to "pray without ceasing." Christ gave us some great examples of this. As He was teaching His disciples to pray, He gave the following illustration:

> Which of you shall have a friend, and go to him at midnight and say to him, "Friend, lend me three loaves; for a friend of mine has come to me on his journey, and I have nothing to set before him"; and he will answer from within and say, "Do not trouble me; the door is now shut, and my children are with me in bed; I cannot rise and give to you anything"? I say to you, though he will not rise and give to him because he is his friend, yet *because of his persistence* he will rise and give him as many as he needs. So I say to you, ask, and it will be given to you; seek, and you will find; knock, and it will be opened to you. (Luke 11:5–9, NKJV, emphasis added)

Sometime later, Jesus told His disciples the following parable:

> "In a certain town there was a judge who neither feared God nor cared what people thought. And there was a widow in that town who kept coming to him with the plea, 'Grant me justice against my adversary.'
>
> "For some time he refused. But finally he said to himself, 'Even though I don't fear God or care what people think, yet *because this widow keeps bothering me*, I will see that she gets justice, so that she won't eventually come and attack me!' "
>
> And the Lord said, "Listen to what the unjust judge says. *And will not God bring about justice for his chosen ones, who cry out to him day and night?* Will he keep putting them off? I tell you, he will see that they get justice, and quickly. However, when the Son of Man comes, will he find faith on the earth?" (Luke 18:2–8, emphasis added)

In Matthew 15:21–28, a Canaanite woman who pleaded with Jesus on behalf of her daughter exemplified this kind of intercession. After Jesus had begun to turn away from her after her first cry because she was not an Israelite, she persisted, kneeling before Him and saying, "Lord, help me!" (Matt 15:25). When Jesus responded by stating, "It is not right to take the children's bread and toss it to the dogs," she did not give up, but said "Yes it is, Lord … even the dogs eat the crumbs that fall from their masters' table" (Matt 15:26–27). And her persistence paid off; Matthew 15:28 records, "Then Jesus answered, 'Woman, you have great faith! Your request is granted.' And her daughter was healed from that very hour" (Matt 15:21–28).

These passages demonstrate the perseverance of those who interceded for others. Those who carried the burden of intercession did not give up. They petitioned with great passion and expectation for results. They had faith and were willing to go the distance.

DING-DONG-DITCH PRAYER

If you are praying for an issue in your life, do you just say one prayer and then move on without giving it another thought? I doubt it. Your burdens are very real to you. You want answers. You want results. So you are passionate about seeking resolution. But E.M. Bounds notes that impatience is often a cause of unanswered prayer. He states, "I think Christians fail so often to get answers to their prayers because they do not wait long enough on God. They just drop down and say a few words, and then jump up and forget it and expect God to answer them. Such praying always reminds me of the small boy ringing his neighbor's door-bell, and then running away as fast as he can go."[2]

When I heard that a brother in Christ with three small children at home had just been laid off from his job, I knew he was praying as he had never prayed before. He must have felt scared, vulnerable, and weak. He was right where God needed him to be—dependent on Him for answers.

When we are truly broken, God can reveal Himself and do what we could never do on our own. The problem is that when we get what we want, we often forget to give Him the glory for the answer—just like the people who did not return to thank Jesus after He had healed them.

ALIGNING OUR REQUESTS TO GOD'S WILL

My wife and I have five children. With three girls and two boys, I spend a lot of time in prayer. In addition to keeping our lives busy, they keep me in humble petition constantly. My wife has also been battling cancer for 14 years. She was diagnosed with thyroid cancer in 1997, but it wasn't identified until it had spread beyond the thyroid and into her blood. The cancer metastasized into forms of blood cancer and was also found in her lungs and cervix. The outcome looked hopeless. During that time, I began praying as I had never prayed before.

Sadly, it is often only when tragedy strikes that we turn to the one who has been knocking on the door of our hearts the whole time. To this day, our family is still praying for my wife's healing and waiting for God to answer, but we have never given up hope. We also recognize that my wife is in a no-lose situation: either I get to keep her and spend the rest of my life on earth with her, or she gets to start eternity with the Father earlier than I will. My prayers began to change as I started spending more time with God.

We often do not receive what we want because we do not ask; and when we ask, far too often we ask outside of God's will (Jas 4:2–3). And so we need to learn how to pray according to God's will. What does He want in every difficult situation? The only way to find out is to spend time with Him.

My intercession for my wife changed from just seeking her physical healing to asking God for His help to raise children who will bring honor to Him—children who will pass on a legacy of faith and be a light to the many generations to come. Now my desire is that the Lord would enable my wife and me to set a new standard for our family heritage. We did not inherit a legacy of faith from our families, but I want more than ever to pass a baton to our five children that will become a memorial stone for them and their children (Deut 6; Psa 78).

Our family has matured in our relationships with the Lord through this battle with cancer, and for that I am grateful. The Scriptures remind us that we will experience hardships (John 16:33; Acts 14:22; 2 Tim 2:3; 4:5; Heb 11, 12:7), but does that mean God turns a deaf ear to our petitions? Absolutely not! He often allows us to go through trials to refine our faith and bring us closer to Him.

If you are praying for a neighbor, a friend, a child, or even a stranger, the Holy Spirit will guide you in your intercession to focus on the areas that really need His intervention. Sometimes the need is crystal clear, but often there are other deep-rooted issues that need to be addressed by the great physician—God. We often focus on the symptoms and not on the issue causing the pain. This is where God does His greatest work in both the person praying and the individual being prayed for. When Moses prayed for Israel, I believe that God was working on him as much as He was working on Israel.

HE HEARS

At the National Day of Prayer Task Force, we truly believe that God hears the prayers of His people and stays His holy hand of judgment on our nation, even if it means diminished punishment in contrast to what we know we deserve. We believe the words of 2 Chronicles 7:14: "If my people, who are called by my name, will humble themselves and pray and seek my face and turn from their wicked ways, then will I hear from heaven, and I will forgive their sin and will heal their land."

God hears His people and responds. But here is the kicker: you may not see the answer to your prayers in your lifetime. Abraham waited 20 years (until he was around 100 years old) for the birth of Isaac in fulfillment of God's promise. The prophets declared the coming of the Messiah, but they did not see Him with their own eyes before they died.

Remember, God is not limited to space and time. He hears our every word and knows the right time to respond. But we have to be diligent in the battle as we pray on the front lines. As James states, "The prayer of a righteous person is powerful and effective" (Jas 5:16).

ENDNOTES

1. William Wilberforce, http://famousquotesandauthors.com.

2. E.M. Bounds, *E.M. Bounds on Prayer* (New Kensington, PA: Whitaker House, 1997).

CHAPTER SIX

RECRUIT TRAINING: THE INTERCESSOR

KATHY BRANZELL

Imagine for a moment that you—just as you are right now—were given the ability to change the world. Not after seeking counseling for your weaknesses, getting a degree from a well-known seminary, working out and preparing with some strength training, but *you*, *right now*.

Imagine that you had the power to expose anything done in darkness with hidden intentions so that all could see (Matt 10:26). What if you had the authority to bless businesses and families as they were getting started or were struggling through difficult times (1 Thess 5:11)? Imagine that you had the ability to comfort and encourage, to embolden and bring healing to the hurting, the struggling, the weak, and the sick (Prov 16:24). What if you could strengthen the military (Isa 41:10) while restoring purity and honor to the Church and the youth of America (2 Cor 6:4–6; 1 Tim 4:12)? Imagine that you had the gift to cast out evil in media and improve education, while joining with fellow believers in those fields to bring honor and glory to God as they worked with a mission-field mindset in their workplaces (Matt 10:8).

What if you had that kind of power? How would you use it? Would you use it? Or would you ignore it, forget you have it, or refuse to use it—even when you knew it would make a difference in the lives of people and in the kingdom of heaven? Of course not! Then why do we forget to pray? Why is prayer sometimes our last resort if it is our most powerful resource?

I was once asked why anyone would want to join the Prayer Movement. Have you watched the news or walked through a school yard lately? Have you gone to the movies? Are you aware that we are at war? Have you heard any statistics about the state of families or the Church recently? If you work: how is business, your boss, or your stock portfolio? How do you feel about those who represent you in government? Is there really justice in America today, and do our courts make decisions that align with Scripture?

Beloved, I ask you this: why would you not see the need or feel an intense desire to join the Prayer Movement? Where does your hope come from (Psa 121:1–8)?

GRASPING AUTHORITY

God has instilled His authority and His power in us through His Spirit, who dwells in us (1 Tim 1:7–8). His power and authority can change the world. It is beyond our comprehension. We were created as Christ's ambassadors (2 Cor 5:20) to represent Him as we walk through life and have dominion over His creation. We were made to talk with the Father about everything good and bad, exciting and scary, thanking Him for the things we encounter here that point us to Him and asking Him to deal with the things that do not.

You may be asking: how can I be meek, as those who shall inherit the earth (Matt 5:5), and stand with authority at the same time? Maybe we misunderstand the word "authority"; it may conjure up pictures of cruelty, pride, or lack of submission, or even stir up memories of someone who ruled over you with an authoritative personality. Let's take a look at a few of the definitions of "authority":

- the right or power to enforce rules or give orders

- the power to act on behalf of somebody else, or official permission to do something
- a source of reliable information on a subject

Authority is given to us—and all believers in Christ, under the reign of God as His children, His servants, and His missionaries here on earth—to go and show the entire world (Mark 16:15) His power, love, mighty hand, wisdom, and grace. Authority is accountability within the Church with mercy; it is teaching God's commands with compassion. It is not judging (Matt 7:1) but demonstrating wisdom from the grace that has been extended to us. We exhibit this not by being cowards but by standing up when fear is telling us to sit down, by advancing when weakness is telling us to retreat. It is the boldness that claims the power of Jesus Christ when the world threatens to crush us; it is fearing God's court more than being taken to court; it is being certain when everyone else doubts. That is the steadfastness that God grows in us when we sign up to be prayer warriors in the Prayer Movement.

Prayer warriors do not hide in foxholes. They do not forget their armor and weapons (Eph 6:13–18) against the evil one, but rather, they enforce the desires of the Commander of His armies, both in heaven and on earth. We must get on our faces before Almighty God and pray with confidence, conviction, and certainty that not only does He hear us, but He will also act upon what we ask in the name of His Son, Jesus Christ. How true is the statement, "You have not because you ask not" (Jas 4:2)? As a friend of God's and not the world, we ask with the motive "Your will, Lord, not mine. On earth as it is in heaven. By your strength and to your glory. That your will is fulfilled, that victory belongs to you."

WHAT'S HOLDING US BACK?

Jesus said in Luke 11:9, "So I say to you: Ask and it will be given to you; seek and you will find; knock and the door will be opened to you."

Why don't we ask? Why don't we seek? Why do we fail to knock? What holds you back from joining the strongest army on earth?

What do you say when a friend comes to you with a problem or your children have a need? What do you do when you see a mother struggling with her children's misbehavior at a store? What is your response to a homeless man asking you for some spare change? What is your reaction when you hear of tragedy, a popular movie star spiraling down the road of destruction, or of corruption in a government or business office? Is your first response to pray for each person and situation, or do you somehow try to fix, dissect, analyze, judge, or even gossip and groan about the situation or person and then move on with your own life?

How do those responses create change? Is the world a better place when we complain?

This may seem like a lot of questions for a book that you turned to for answers, but questions can help you start at the beginning—to know where you stand and why. Many people do not pray for others for a variety of reasons, from "I have so many problems of my own that I can't even think about other people's problems" to "I am afraid I will pray for the wrong thing; I might not know the whole story or have all the facts" or "Will it hurt my witness if God does not do what I ask Him?" Or maybe you have so many things to do that you are just too busy. (Ron Wilson at Focus on the Family sees the word "busy" as an acronym for "being under Satan's yolk.")

What strongholds in our lives make us weak-willed instead of warriors? Here are a few.

Stronghold #1: I have too many problems of my own to worry about other people's problems.

First, consider Luke 12:25–26: "And which of you by worrying can add a single hour to his life's span? If then you cannot do even a very little thing, why do you worry about other matters?" (NASB). Worrying accomplishes nothing. It may even set you back with fatigue, illness, emotional outbursts, and more.

The Prayer Movement presses on; it does not experience setbacks. The very best way to get your mind off your own problems is to start praying for other people. Follow the words of 1 John 4:7: "Beloved, let us love one another, for love is from God; and everyone who loves is born of God and knows God." Lifting others up will lift you up. Praying for others puts your own problems into perspective and sets your heart in the right place as you "love your neighbor as yourself." Nothing cures a pity party like praise.

Focusing on a mighty, immeasurable, all-powerful, loving God reminds us that we have an awesome Father who loves us and knows and wants what is best for us. He has all the answers and all the resources we need.

Stronghold #2: I'm experiencing doubt.

When we pray, it's easy to fall into doubt, to ask whether prayer will really help. James 1:6–8 addresses this very issue: "But when you ask, you must believe and not doubt, because the one who doubts is like a wave of the sea, blown and tossed by the wind. That person should not expect to receive anything from the Lord. Such a person is double-minded and unstable in all they do."

The next time you find yourself held back from praying fully by doubt, remember these words from Mark 11:23: "Truly I tell you, if anyone says to this mountain, 'Go, throw yourself into the sea,' and does not doubt in his heart but believes that what they say will happen, it will be done for them."

Stronghold #3: I might not have all the facts, and I am not sure what to pray for.

Don't be afraid that you do not know all the facts or that there might be more to the story; God has all the facts. As Romans 8:26 states, "In the same way, the Spirit helps us in our weakness. We do not know what we ought to pray for, but the Spirit himself intercedes for us through wordless groans."

When we pray with a pure heart, in God's will, we do not have to worry about praying for the wrong thing. God always does the right thing—the *best* thing. And the best thing we can do is pray. As James 1:5 states, "If any of you lacks wisdom, you should ask God, who gives generously to all without finding fault, and it will be given to you."

Stronghold #4: I just want to "fix" things when people come to me with their problems.

Love and compassion for others makes us desire to fix problems, or at least help with them. Rather than praying, your first reaction may be to leap into action using your resources and connections to try to fix other people's lives. Of course, trying to help other people solve their problems—with a pure heart and good intent—is kind, but jumping into action before you pray over people and their situation is kind of crazy.

God not only knows all the facts about a situation, He also has all the answers and resources for every single person on the face of this earth. As Luke 12:27–31 states:

> Consider how the wild flowers grow. They do not labor or spin. Yet I tell you, not even Solomon in all his splendor was dressed like one of these. If that is how God clothes the grass of the field, which is here today, and tomorrow is thrown into the fire, how much more will He clothe you—you of little faith! And do not set your heart on what you will eat or drink; do not worry about it. For the pagan world runs after all such things, and your Father knows that you need them. But seek his kingdom, and these things will be given to you as well.

You and I do not have all the answers, but God does. So why would we go anywhere else but to Him?

As the president of a Christian ministry for educators, I receive hundreds of emails every day regarding personal and professional prayer requests. So how is it that days and weeks later, we receive praise and thanksgiving reports from our schools reporting resolution to thousands of problems? *Prayer!* Week after week, God has heard our prayers, and we rejoice with educators and schools across this nation as we hear how God has healed the sick, changed the troubled student, brought unity to a torn school, and talked sense into an intoxicated parent terrorizing a campus. Prayer has prompted God to fix broken systems, change the decisions of the corrupt, bring resources to impoverished districts, stop violence and tragedy, and increase success. God has answered so many prayers and worked so many miracles that there are too many to count. In my own strength and with my own resources, I could not have helped the thousands of people who have come to our ministry for help. But with God, all things are possible (Matt 19:26).

Stronghold #5: I don't really know this person.

God may prompt you to pray for a person who you have never met. It may be someone you see crying in a grocery store or a celebrity being chased around by the media. It may be a child in a picture or a government official who you do not even agree with. It may be someone who was rude to you on the highway or a receptionist with a sweet smile and an energetic attitude. It may be a worker who never arrives on time or a military plane full of soldiers headed to the front lines of a war. But we do not need to know all the people we pray for—God already does. He knows us all through and through—"the very hairs of your head" (Luke 12:7)—every need, desire, hurt, fear, gift, and family member.

God knows everyone we pray for; He created them. Consider Psalm 139:1–5: "You have searched me, Lord, and you know me. You know when I sit and when I rise; you perceive my thoughts from afar. You discern my going out and my lying down; you are familiar with all my ways. Before a word is on my tongue you, Lord, know it completely." Nothing escapes His attention or gets past Him. He does not get distracted, nor can He be tricked or outsmarted.

Proverbs 21:30 says, "There is no wisdom, no insight, no plan that can succeed against the Lord." Our job is to just make sure that no prayer opportunity goes unprayed.

Stronghold #6: "Well, they got what they deserved."

Friends, what God's word says is enough for me: "The Lord is compassionate and gracious, slow to anger, abounding in love. He will not always accuse, nor will He harbor His anger forever; He does not treat us as our sins deserve or repay us according to our iniquities. For as high as the heavens are above the earth, so great is His love for those who fear Him; as far as the east is from the west, so far has He removed our transgressions from us" (Psa 103:8–13).

I thank God every day that He does not treat me as my sins deserve. How could I ever ask for His mercy for myself and His judgment for another? Instead, we should remember Luke 6:37, which states, "Do not judge, and you will not be judged. Do not condemn, and you will not be condemned. Forgive, and you will be forgiven."

I have been forgiven much, and therefore I will forgive much. I am human, and so are the rest of the people I walk this earth with. And as 1 Corinthians 4:3–5 states, "I care very little if I am judged by you or by any human court; indeed, I do not even judge myself. … It is the Lord who judges me. Therefore judge nothing before the appointed time; wait until the Lord comes. He will bring to light what is hidden in darkness and will expose the motives of the heart" (1 Cor 4:3–5).

Who am I that He would love me, forgive me, and think loving thoughts toward me? Who am I that I would not want that for all of humankind? Second Peter 3:9 says, "The Lord is not slow in keeping his promise, as some understand slowness. Instead he is patient with you, not wanting anyone to perish, but everyone to come to repentance." Who am I not to desire the same?

Stronghold #7: Does God really expect me to pray for my "enemies"?

Throughout the Old Testament, God made it clear that He desires people to pray on behalf of one another. For example, after God allowed Satan to afflict Job in an effort to shake his faith, Job's friends accused him of sin, increasing his suffering. Nevertheless, God instructed Job to pray over his friends so that He would not deal with them according to their folly (Job 42:7–9), and Job obeyed.

In 1 Kings 13, King Jeroboam stretched out his hand to harm the man of God sent to prophesy against him, and his hand shriveled up and could not be pulled back. The king then asked the man of God to pray for his hand to be restored. Jeroboam did not ask him to pray for his soul or for forgiveness, but as a sign of faith in God and God's glory, the prophet prayed for the evil king, and his hand was restored.

Jesus expressed that same wish in the New Testament: "You have heard that it was said, 'Love your neighbor and hate your enemy.' But I tell you: Love your enemies and pray for those who persecute you, that you may be sons of your Father in heaven" (Matt 5:43–44). And on the cross, Christ cried out for forgiveness for those who had plotted against Him, betrayed Him, and crucified Him. The example has been given; it is for us to follow.

These strongholds chain us down and hold us captive by the deceiver. Pray them away. Break their bonds with the supernatural power of God in you, implementing the freedom given to you by Christ on the cross.

ONWARD

The role of intercessor may seem mysterious to some and inefficient to others. How many times have you heard someone say, "Well, all we can do is pray"? I pray that by now you have begun to grasp the incredible power and profit that come through prayer alone. We are more than conquerors through Christ. If we expect to do anything to improve situations, circumstances, and souls, we must start with prayer. It is only in being still (Psa 46:10) in faith-filled prayer that we can move mountains.

Onward, Christian soldier! The Prayer Movement is on the move. It is about advancing the kingdom, taking a leap of faith. It is pressing on to finish the race. As a fellow member of the Prayer Movement, you *can* change the world.

CHAPTER SEVEN

BOOT CAMP: MOBILIZING THE CHURCH

DION ELMORE

Shortly after Jesus ascended into heaven, the early disciples made the trip back to Jerusalem to gather and wait. They knew that something was going to happen. Jesus had instructed them to wait for power. But what exactly did that mean? What kind of power? They had walked with Jesus, they had observed Him pray, and they had participated in the miracles that He worked. But they really didn't understand what was going to happen next.

In my own experience, I've learned the same lesson. When I don't know what to do next, I wait and pray. That's exactly what they did: they returned to the upper room, and as Acts 1:14 puts it, "They all continued with one accord in prayer and supplication."

Imagine being there with this ragtag assembly of fishermen, tax collectors, tradesmen, farmers, fathers, mothers, and religious leaders—a group of ordinary people who found themselves right in the middle of something extraordinary. They were just praying and waiting for God's promise, His Holy Spirit. Receiving power meant that their lives would be dramatically seized, forever changed, and radically redirected. Once hindered by fear, apprehension, and misunderstanding, this group would soon become a very powerful army of witnesses. Lives would be transformed and miracles would be performed. The news would spread rapidly, the gospel would be shared, and thousands upon thousands of new disciples would be added to the Church every week.

MAINTAINING THE MAIN THINGS

In those early days, the disciples would be flooded with opportunities to participate in God's work, and then to see instant results. No time to prepare, no time to reflect, no time to even think about what was happening to them. The Holy Spirit had fallen upon them. As they sought God's guidance and struggled to accommodate all of the growth, they settled on a very simple ministry plan. They pledged to keep focus on the main things. With determination, they set out to focus on four key areas. In Acts 2:42, these are outlined for us: they "devoted themselves to the apostles' teaching and to fellowship, to the breaking of bread and to prayer."

The apostles understood their priorities and when challenged with waiting tables, they, in the wisdom of God, chose instead to focus on giving themselves "continually to prayer and to the ministry of the word" (Acts 6:4). By maintaining their focus, they remained plugged in to God. As a result, they maintained an intentional focus that alerted them to the needs and opportunities around them.

STAYING ENGAGED WITH THE BASICS

It's all pretty basic, isn't it? We, the 21st century church, can take a few lessons from the founders. As we mobilize the Church of Jesus Christ today, what are we focusing on? What are the current trends in the Church today? What are we busy doing? Let's compare our activities to the activities of the early disciples. Are we focused on teaching the word of God? Are we in the business of developing intimate relationships and promoting fellowship among believers? Are we praying steadfast, continual prayer?

We may do those things, but how intentional and effective are we at accomplishing them? You see, the most basic things are the things we seem to become the most bored with. We need to be honest in our assessment before we can be effective. We should ask ourselves these questions:

- Are we *steadfastly* praying over every area of your churches ministry?
- Are we *steadfastly* seeking God's direction?
- Are we *steadfastly* asking for His protection?
- Are we *steadfastly* praying against every stronghold of the enemy that God reveals to us?

The early church's use of the word "steadfastly" indicates that they believed it was not only important but *essential* to keep these fundamentals in place. The idea is to devote ourselves continually and diligently to these things. They understood that without the foundation of truth, relationship, and prayer, there could be no real lasting impact in the Church or through the Church. The world was against them, the devil was roaming about, and they had to seek wisdom and direction from the Lord.

Things really haven't changed. The foundations of a sound church are still the same. Every church that intends to be about God's business with power must attend to these basics continually. We are still resisting the devil and storming the gates of hell. And we still need wisdom and direction from the Lord.

BEGINNING WITH A BURDEN

A number of years ago, as I was praying about the possibility of planting a new church, I kept running into the first chapter of Nehemiah. Over and over, at conference after conference, speakers drew my attention to the same verse: Nehemiah 1:4. Eventually, that verse captured my focus and led me to understand that powerful ministry grows from a heart burdened to pray. Let's take a look at Nehemiah 1:1–4:

It came to pass in the month of Kislev … Hanani, one of my brothers, came from Judah with some other men, and I questioned them about the Jewish remnant that survived the exile, and also about Jerusalem. They said to me, "Those who survived the exile and are back in the province are in great trouble and disgrace. The wall of Jerusalem is also broken down, and its gates have been burned with fire."

When I heard these things, I sat down and wept. For some days I mourned and fasted and prayed before the God of heaven.

Before he received the devastating news about the wall of Jerusalem, Nehemiah was doing quite well. But, as often happens, along came a burden from God. Nehemiah stopped what he was doing, listened, and then wept and mourned for many days. The Lord had captured his heart. Here's a principal worth remembering: a captured heart leads to compassionate prayer.

Every major work that God prepares for us, He also prepares *us* for. The problem is that the preparation process is often difficult. It's uncomfortable to ask God to break our hearts over the plight of people. But if we look through His eyes, we'll begin to see a tremendous need all around us—need that will compel us to pray. In every city, every neighborhood, there are people who are in captivity, ensnared by the world, tempted in their flesh, and blinded by the devil. They are in "great trouble and disgrace" (Neh 1:3).

If, like Nehemiah, God has captured our hearts and we are compelled to fervent prayer, what should we do next? What did Nehemiah do? He mobilized. Nehemiah began to prepare through prayer. He sought wisdom, prayed for favor, and began taking steps to follow God's prompting. Even though Nehemiah had never been to Jerusalem, the plight of the people became personal to him.

If we have been compelled to pray, then we will be mobilized into action. Let's assess the needs and plight of the people in the community in which we live. Is there a need for us, for our churches, to rise up together and pray? To mobilize and take action? To mount up an attack on the strongholds of our common enemies? To take back lost ground, and to build a wall of protection around those who are desperately in need? Of course there is.

PREPARATION FOR ACTION

The Apostle Paul offers an illustration of the mobilized power of prayer to the early church in Corinth. Attempting to teach these early believers the effectiveness of intentional prayer, Paul instructs them that "the weapons of our warfare are not carnal but mighty in God for pulling down strongholds, casting down arguments and every high thing that exalts itself against the knowledge of God" (2 Cor 10:4 NKJV). The weapon of prayer is powerful and effective. It is a weapon that, when focused against the strongholds of bondage, sin, arguments, and arrogance, literally tears them apart.

The early church formulated its strategy and tactics based on their observations of the strongholds in people's lives. God would reveal strongholds, and they would pray against them. They realized that the "principalities and powers" that they battled against were extremely busy fortifying existing strongholds and continually beginning construction on new ones. They also realized that the weapons they possessed were mighty in God. They had the weaponry, but they were not very skilled when it came to planning and carrying out warfare in prayer. In order to become skilled, they needed training and practice.

DEVELOPING AND MOBILIZING PEOPLE IN THE CHURCH

When I first began working in ministry, I spent a lot of time trying to encourage God's people to pray, and I discovered that I had no power to place a burden of prayer within people. I knew that there was power in prayer, but I wasn't quite sure how to mobilize people to pray or how to get them to take action. I found relief when I read Ephesians 4, which teaches that a pastor's role is not to incite people to pray or ensure that they do pray; a pastor's role is simply to equip the people to serve while allowing the Holy Spirit to impart to them a heart to pray and the desire to serve.

Like a drill sergeant, pastors are given the role of equipping new recruits and giving them the tools they need to become effective soldiers. And we are definitely engaged in a war—a war against the world, the flesh, and the devil. All of us are drafted into the Lord's service, issued spiritual armor and weaponry, and given instruction in effective engagement.

Equipping saints is a daunting task. Imagine that you are a drill sergeant in the army who is responsible for preparing men and women for battle, for taking raw recruits and turning them into the best fighting force on the face of the earth. You would have the best resources at your disposal, the best weapons, and the best equipment, and you could have as many months as you need. But you only have 30 to 45 minutes, once a week, to train them. And, by the way, these soldiers may not show up every week—after all, they are pretty busy with their personal lives. Would you take the challenge?

That's exactly the challenge that pastors face. In a sense, they have devoted their lives to training a "volunteer" Christian army: men and women with every physical and spiritual resource at their disposal, equipped with the most powerful weapons in the universe, and against whom no effective weapons have ever been formed. These men and women are able to battle with every principality and power, no matter how ferocious. And their assault will make the foundations of the gates of hell tremble and the walls crumble. But pastors are expected to train their army in just 45 minutes a week, 52 Sundays each year, or as often as their troops choose to show up. (If that is every Sunday, that's still only 39 hours a year—less time than most people spend at their jobs each week.) Without the Holy Spirit's involvement, this would be an impossible task.

So how do we mobilize the Church to pray? This may sound simplistic, but the most effective way that I've found is to pray for them to have a burden for prayer. Pray for the people. Pray for them to understand the resources that they have available. Pray for a burden like Nehemiah had. Pray that the Holy Spirit will teach and train them as your pastors do the work of equipping them. Pray that they would understand that prayer is the "powerhouse" of the Church. Turn up the heat on the saints so they can turn up the heat against the world, the flesh, and the devil.

TURNING UP THE HEAT

Charles Spurgeon understood this principal well. *Our Daily Bread* shared this episode:

> Five young college students were spending a Sunday in London, so they went to hear the famed C.H. Spurgeon preach. While waiting for the doors to open, the students were greeted by a man who asked, "Gentlemen, let me show you around. Would you like to see the heating plant of this church?" They were not particularly interested, for it was a hot day in July. But they didn't want to offend the stranger, so they consented. The young men were taken down a stairway, a door was quietly opened, and their guide whispered, "This is our heating plant." Surprised, the students saw 700 people bowed in prayer, seeking a blessing on the service that was soon to begin in the auditorium above. Softly closing the door, the gentleman then introduced himself. It was none other than Charles Spurgeon.[1]

The term "Boiler Room Prayer" was coined to describe the real power plant of a powerful, praying church. At the Metropolitan Tabernacle where Spurgeon served as pastor, there were hundreds of praying saints in the "boiler room" crying out to God during every service. They prayed for salvation to come, for freedom from bondage, and for power over sin. And God answered their prayer. They prayed for their pastor—that God would empower him and use him in a mighty way. And God answered their prayer. Faithfully, week after week, they prayed for the young men who were training at the Pastors College and serving at that church and others that they were supporting. And God answered their prayer.

I had the privilege of sitting next to Rick Warren, a best-selling author and pastor, at a dinner a couple of years ago. We were talking about spiritual heritage, and he shared with me that his great-grandfather was one of those young men trained at the Pastors College in London. He was sent to the United States and became a circuit-riding preacher. Rick's father was also a pastor, and today Rick himself is an influential evangelical pastor. I believe that the prayers prayed by those "boiler room" saints over 100 years ago are still affecting the world today through the ministry of Rick Warren and others who are descendants of the blessings of prayers prayed years before their birth.

How far reaching are your prayers? Consider the impact your prayers can have on the lives of your children and grandchildren. I've experienced this sort of impact directly. I am descended from a long line of believers on my father's side of the family. While I didn't have a great-grandfather who graduated from Spurgeon's Pastors College, I did have grandparents who prayed. My grandmother, Millie, was one of those prayer warriors. A simple farm girl from Iowa, she and my grandfather raised a family of 11 during the depression and World War II era. Life was hard, but she had great faith. And she prayed. From her 11 children, only one or two strayed away from the faith. The majority of her grandchildren are believers, and several are involved in ministry.

What do you want your heritage to be? As we pray for our young kids, we usually don't think to pray for their children. But we need to. We need to pray for our children and our children's children, to pray that God would use them in mighty ways—that He would raise up a spiritual army from our family.

SPANNING TIME AND SPACE

Consider the sphere of influence that you have through your prayers. I've seen prayer not only resonate through time but also span continents. We are waging war with principalities and powers—not just in our geographic area, but in other nations as well. Through the power of God and prayer, you can mount an offensive against strongholds all over the world. Imagine the impact you can have beyond your home town. I challenge you: set your sights beyond your own area, your own family, your own nation.

In my current prayer list, I pray for pastors, missionaries, and friends on every continent (including Antarctica at times). I have intimate knowledge of the needs in many nations because I am connected with the saints of God there. When you have a vested interest in the lives of others around the world, you gain an interest in the unique needs and challenges that they have. You begin to understand the spiritual warfare that they face, and this better equips you to pray for others as God brings them onto your prayer lists. As time goes on, you begin to not just sympathize but *empathize* with these precious people. And your prayers begin to take shape, passionately aimed at the heart of their needs. Then, spiritual strongholds begin to fall.

THE DEVELOPMENT OF AN OFFENSIVE MINDSET

When your motivation in prayer comes from love and empathy, you will naturally become more intentional. Your warfare against the strongholds of the enemy in prayer will not be defensive, but it will shift to outright campaigns against darkness that you will be leading.

You will no longer respond to attacks, but you will mount up on the offensive. You will press against everything that is not of God, and you will experience victory in battle like you've never seen.

God sent Joshua on the offensive to take the promised land. He promised that the land would be taken. He promised that He would be with him. More than once, though, the Lord had to encourage Joshua. Why? Because he was human. Like you and me, he suffered from uncertainty. He battled with unbelief. The words that God spoke to him, the promises He gave to Joshua, resonate in my mind:

> No one will be able to stand against you all the days of your life. As I was with Moses, so I will be with you; I will not leave you nor forsake you. Be strong and courageous, because you will lead these people to inherit the land I swore to their ancestors to give them. Be strong and very courageous. Be careful to obey all the law which my servant Moses gave you; do not turn from it to the right or to the left, that you may be successful wherever you go. Keep this Book of the Law always on your lips; meditate on it day and night, so that you may be careful to do everything written in it. Then you will be prosperous and successful. Have I not commanded you? Be strong and courageous. Do not be afraid; do not be discouraged, for the LORD your God will be with you wherever you go. (Josh 1:5–9)

If God is for us, who can be against us? (This is a rhetorical question—you already know the answer.) As the Lord was with Joshua, He will be with you and me.

When we resolve to heed His word, He will resolve to prosper our prayers wherever we go. We can pray for India, and God will prosper our prayers. We can pray for China, and God will prosper our prayers. We are commanded by God to pray, and we can take the encouragement from God's living, powerful word. Listen to these words as though your Father in Heaven were speaking them directly to you. Hear what He says, and go on the offensive. "Have I not commanded you? Be strong and of good courage; do not be afraid, nor be dismayed, for the Lord your God is with you wherever you go" (Josh 1:9).

ENDNOTES

1.   *Our Daily Bread*, April 24

CHAPTER EIGHT

STRATEGIC PLANNING: APPROACHING PRAYER INTENTIONALLY

DION ELMORE

very branch of the military has a basic training program to equip their recruits with the skill sets that they will need in order to carry out their objectives in warfare. They are issued a field manual, an exhaustive volume created for the purpose of training in the finer points of strategy and activity in war.

I came across a copy of the *Army Field Manual* a while back and noticed many parallels between their physical warfare and our spiritual warfare. Learning how to evaluate targets, develop a strategy for attack, and assess damage done are essential whether you're waging war in the physical or spiritual realm. Every soldier in service for their country must learn to wage war.

When I compare Christians to earthly soldiers, I see most engaged in worldly pursuits, like a reservist. Those involved in the reserves aren't full-time soldiers, they're citizen soldiers—an army in reserve, ready at any time to be called up when needed. Whether full time or reserve, the requirements for training are the same: every soldier must go through basic training, and every soldier must have continual training along the way to remain sharp and skilled.

As a church, our basic training occurs on the job. Most are citizen soldiers who have a responsibility to work by day and fight by night.

For a period of time, we must lay down our earthly pursuits and train for battle. We must keep our field manual close at hand. We must work hard to gain the training and knowledge we'll need to be effective.

KNOW YOUR ENEMY

During our training, we will learn the tactics that we will need to win. We will intimately learn the wiles and weapons of our enemy. I remember my father telling me that in basic training for the Navy in World War II, he had to memorize the shapes and sounds of enemy aircraft. They had to be able to identify an aircraft by their silhouettes and decibels so that the enemy would not be able to sneak up on them. In the 1986 Clint Eastwood movie, *Heartbreak Ridge,* the seasoned gunnery sergeant, Tom "Gunny" Highway, is training his recruits when he stops, pulls out an automatic rifle, and begins to shoot live ammunition over their heads. His recruits dive to the ground, and Gunny Highway speaks these memorable words: "This is the AK-47 assault rifle, the preferred weapon of your enemy. It makes a distinctive sound when fired at you. So remember it." In order to be acquainted with your enemy's weapons, you must be exposed to them.

Knowing the tactics and the patterns that the enemy of our soul uses will be essential in recognizing an attack when it occurs. The patterns of our flesh are consistent, and they are similar to those of our fathers and our fathers' fathers. And the devil generally isn't original in his tactics. If your grandfather struggled with pride, your father struggled with pride, and you're struggling with pride, guess what tactic the enemy will use on you? Guard against your weakest area because you will be attacked at your weakest point. Recognize your weaknesses, your vulnerabilities—the parts of you that are "open to assault."

VULNERABILITY ASSESSMENT

How vulnerable are you? Have you put on the "whole armor of God"? Are you practicing using your weapons? Are you skilled in defending yourself against the "fiery darts" that are continually being launched in your direction?

Most losses in battle occur—and most setbacks in ministry happen—because we have not been more thorough in our self-examination. Along with our own examination, with the psalmist in Psalm 26:2, we cry out to the Lord, "Test me, O Lord, and try me; examine my mind and my heart." The purpose is to reveal any "wicked way" or weakness that may be in us. When we cry out, the Lord reveals our vulnerable places. We can then deal with them and strengthen any area that is weak.

Why is this important? Because the enemy will attack us in your area of greatest weakness. As we seek the Lord's examination in prayer, He will not only expose the area of greatest weakness in our life, but He will also expose the weaknesses in the lives of those we're praying for. As the Lord exposes areas of weakness, we should begin to pray specifically for those areas, carefully focusing our prayers.

Overestimating the strength of our opposition can be equally destructive. We know from God's word that any of *their* weapons are ultimately ineffective against those who are in Christ. When we take action in prayer, we must understand that "'No weapon formed against you shall prosper, and every tongue which rises against you in judgment you shall condemn. This is the heritage of the servants of the Lord, and their righteousness is from Me" (Isa 54:17). Psalm 27:1 proclaims that "the Lord is my light and my salvation; whom shall I fear? The Lord is the strength of my life; of whom shall I be afraid?" Romans 8:31 asks us a rhetorical question, "What, then, shall we say to these things? If God is for us, who can be against us?" Not angels, nor principalities, nor powers. Those are great odds!

TARGETING

In the *Army Field Manual*, the objective of targeting is determining "what to attack, how to acquire those targets, and when those targets are acquired, how to attack them in a way that disrupts, delays or limits the enemy's ability to achieve his objectives." How would you like to be so focused in your prayers that you know just what to pray for, what to pray against, and how to "disrupt, delay or limit the enemy's ability to achieve his objectives"? You *can* be that focused. By choosing a few key areas to focus your attention on, you can sharply increase your effectiveness in prayer.

To effectively target needs, challenges, and strongholds with our prayers, we must know what we're aiming at. If we fail to aim, we will fail to hit our target every time. So what should our prayer targets be? What should make up the content and direction of our prayers? Over the last several years, I've identified a simple strategy to help me keep my prayers on target. I also use the same pattern to teach others how to effectively target their prayers.

The first troops to be sent into any conflict are the scouts. Their job is reconnaissance: the exploration conducted to gain information. One of the greatest reconnaissance tools in your arsenal are your ears. People will reveal to you in conversation the strongholds that they are fighting against. You simply have to listen. I want to encourage you to buy a small notebook and make a habit of carrying that and a pen or pencil with you at all times. Begin to strike up conversations with people, take out your pad and pen, and ask them if you might make a few notes because you'd like to pray for them. You will be amazed how they will open up simply because they know that you are sincerely interested in their needs.

While many prayer needs will be specific to that person and their situation, I've found that you can ask some very simple probing questions that will help you identify their prayer needs. Have you ever heard of the Pareto Principle? You may know it better as the 80/20 rule. It states that for many events in life, 80 percent of the effects come from 20 percent of the causes. In other words, if you can identify and address the 20 percent of the causes, 80 percent of the effects or issues will disappear.

Over the last 20 years of ministry, I've been able to identify several key life issues that seem to generate about 80 percent of people's life struggles:

- Life purpose
- Communication
- Relationship
- Marriage
- Parenting
- Finances
- Sexuality

The list isn't exhaustive by any means, but it is a good guideline for gauging how and where people are struggling. The best way to help others deal with these strongholds is to listen and ask questions. As you show sincere interest in people's lives and let them know that you are going to be praying for them, you'll be amazed at their responsiveness.

Imagine this scenario: one of your coworkers is struggling with her marriage, and the key issues are communication and finances. If you ask if you can pray for her, 9 out of 10 times she'll say, "Sure." As you begin to pray, make a point to check in and ask how things are progressing. As you focus on praying for these areas, you can also encourage her with tools to help her understand how to get these areas under control. You will see great victories in her life.

You can begin to pray for whole communities this way—that people would find hope and purpose, that they would be freed from the bondage of debt and from sexual immorality. If 80 percent of people struggle with these issues, imagine how much good targeting these areas would do in freeing many in our communities from bondage.

Another place to target strongholds is in our communities. To do this, we must become students of the news. When we watch our local news or read our local paper, what do we see? I look for patterns and areas that are consistently in the news. I know which parts of town have the highest instances of drugs, crime, gang activity, and prostitution. I can also tell you which areas of our community have the most affluence and influence. I pay attention to prevalent issues in individual school districts. I know the civic leaders by name, the heads of the school districts, the community influencers and power brokers. I pay attention to the economy and its effects on the individual neighborhoods—which schools are closing, how many families are affected, which neighborhoods have the most for sale signs. If we pay attention, we will always have areas, issues, and people to specifically target with our prayers.

Alongside these more common issues, there seems to be an almost endless list of other areas of bondage that exist in people's lives. Over the last 10 years, I've seen a marked increase in the struggles that people experience. The most common concerns I've encountered are mental and emotional issues like depression, bipolar disorder, and panic and anxiety disorders, as well as the mental and emotional effects of the drugs associated with their treatment. Areas of sexual sin like fornication, adultery, and pornography are very common strongholds, with substance addictions to alcohol, illegal and prescription drugs following close behind.

As you become more familiar with the needs and strongholds in your area, ask the Lord to reveal His heart and desires to you through prayer. Every area of ungodliness in our personal lives and in our communities grieves the heart of God. His will is that all evil is rooted out and that His light and righteousness rule and reign. Begin holding a regular prayer meeting where everyone who has a burden to pray can attend. Together in one accord, you can pray and seek direction as to which strongholds He would have you attack together.

PREPARING YOUR PLAN TO PRAY

An old saying goes, "If you fail to plan, you plan to fail." Prayer is no different. In order to experience consistent victory in intercessory prayer, we must make ourselves a prayer plan—a scheme or method of

STRATEGIC PLANNING: APPROACHING PRAYER INTENTIONALLY

doing. We must prepare in advance and be organized. In our plan, we should include prayers for our leaders, churches, country, community, work, school, families, friends, neighbors, coworkers, and whoever else the Lord brings to our minds.

Step 1: Develop a Prayer Plan

Most Christians are free-form in their prayer life. They pray general prayers at general times and in general places. They don't want to be constrained by a plan; they want to go with the flow as the Holy Spirit reveals what they are to pray for.

This sounds very spiritual on the surface, but when you walk with true prayer warriors, you find that there is always a method to their praying. You also find that they are very disciplined in carrying out their plan. To have a developed a strategic plan doesn't take away from the Spirit's leading; rather, it enhances it. You can be led by the Spirit and stay on task; it's not an either/or choice but a both/and approach.

When we are praying specifically, we are continually bringing to mind, adding to, and subtracting from the prayer needs that are in front of us. Much like memorization of Scripture, continued repetition of prayer helps keep the most important things at the forefront of our minds. The things we think about become the things that we focus on. Inspiration is the first part, and then comes the tough part: acting on what we know.

Step 2: Work the Plan

Most people who are determined prayer warriors find that prayer is a true discipline and labor when pursued with passion. The difficulty for us comes in the form of being faithful to pray. Effective, fervent prayer—specific and directed prayer—is not easy. When we engage in intercessory prayer for others, we move ahead with the understanding that there are specific targets to hit and that keeping the pressure on those targets will take time.

The Roman armies had a long-term strategy for tearing down strongholds. They would scout around a walled fortress and look for its weaknesses. Then, they would bring in supplies and establish a camp around the stronghold. After this, they would lay siege to it while simultaneously building towers and ramps. They used this strategy when they attacked Jerusalem in AD 70. According to Josephus, a Jewish historian who observed this attack from the Roman side as a prisoner, the siege was successful, but only after five months of severe fighting.

The harder we pray, the harder the battle will be. The devil and his demons don't like having their encampments routed by prayer, and they will most certainly retaliate. As the counterattacks come, we must respond with greater intensity and effort to keep the offensive going. We must keep up the attack and use every weapon at our disposal. There will be seasons when you see victory, and there will be seasons when you feel as though the victory belongs to the enemy. It's all about perseverance and faithfulness. Your charge is to pray.

Step 3: Develop a Regular Prayer List

Once we've developed our prayer plan, assessed the needs, identified strongholds, and realized that this is a long-term commitment to be faithful, we must create our list. Keeping lists of prayer needs is a simple way to stay on target and measure progress; keep track of who, what, and when, and then add what happened. I'd suggest always having your Bible, a notebook to write your lists on, and a pencil or pen when you pray.

Record notes on your list. If you take notes from your scouting exercises and any letters or newsletters you get from your missionary friends, you will end up with a scrapbook of notes about your community needs. Then begin to pray. Pray as the Holy Spirit leads. He will give you supernatural insight into other things you've not written down; when He does, write those things down and add them to your list. Remember, prayer is dynamic, and it is always changing. You should always be ready to modify your prayer list. As your list begins to grow, you will need to set aside dedicated time to pray each day. Get into the habit and develop the discipline.

Step 4: Take Time to Pray

Time is a precious commodity. We speak in concepts of "spending" or "saving" when we talk about it. Like money, we never seem to have enough—we always wish we had more. Everyone has the same amount given to them each week, but some people accomplish so much with theirs, and others accomplish very little.

Priorities dictate how we choose to spend our time. We live out what we value, and our lives speak volumes about what is truly important to us. As Christians, we know that the word of God is critical to our health and well-being, and we know that we must have strong relationships with other believers. We also know that prayer is the key to having a vibrant relationship with Jesus and having a powerful ministry toward others. If these things are all true, why is it so difficult to give our time to these things?

It really boils down to two things: misplaced priorities and a lack of discipline. For most of us, "discipline" is not a pleasant word; when we hear it, we think of punishment. But instead, we should be thinking of faithfulness. We all live in a busy culture, and we lead very busy lives; in fact, busyness is probably one of the greatest enemies of prayer. For many of us, prayer may mean that we have to get up earlier or stay up later to get time alone with God. Unfortunately, this usually works to our disadvantage, and we become tired. If we're tired, prayer becomes increasingly difficult.

The best way to work around tiredness is to plan your prayer times for some time during the day when you're wide awake. As you make time in your schedule and prioritize your time to pray, you will by necessity eliminate many of the things that are presently consuming you. Are you a morning person or a night owl? When do you have the most energy? What times do you usually chose to do the things that you like most? We often chose to do things we love during our most energetic times. Who would go to a movie at the end of the day when they're fatigued? They might fall asleep. Unfortunately, that is exactly when most of us remember to pray, and we end up offering snoring instead of supplication. Give God the best time of your day. Pray with your spouse or friends. Choose an evening during the week and gather together.

And remember this: we don't really have much time. The days are growing more and more evil, life is becoming more dangerous and difficult, and we're not getting any younger. I periodically stroll through a local cemetery to regain perspective. I typically choose the older graves because many of them list more information about the individuals and families buried there. These people all lived their lives like we do. They were beloved fathers, mothers, sisters, brothers, sons, and daughters. They had loves and dreams, work and troubles, just like you and me. And the only thing left of them is an old stone with a few words. This is how it will be for us all. James made a powerful statement: "For what is your life? It is even a vapor that appears for a little time and then vanishes away" (Jas 4:14 NKJV). Don't let your life vanish away without accomplishing what God has placed you here on the earth to do. Choose to pray, and He will bless your investment.

Step 5: Journal Answers to Prayer

A soldier wouldn't be worth his weight if he didn't keep track of his victories. No soldier would report back to his commanding officer and say, "I'm not sure what I hit, but I think I hit something." In warfare and prayer, we need to track our victories. As you pray, pay attention to how the Lord begins to answer, and record what you observe in your prayer journal.

Keeping track of God's answers brings encouragement. The Lord had the children of Israel erect stone monuments to remind them of what He had accomplished in their midst. The people in the nations surrounding the Israelites may not have observed the parting of the Red Sea, but they did hear about it; and when they did, the result was a fear of the God of Israel. When we recognize how God has answered prayer, we remain encouraged, people hear and realize who our God is, and we continue to pray.

As we journal, we must always remember that prayer takes time. If we are praying against strongholds that the enemy has controlled for a long time, it may take a while to pull them down. I've been praying for some people for over 20 years. In some cases, I'm still waiting to see God move, but I haven't seen any change. The issue for me is not just seeing the change, but my dedication to these people over time. Even though it's been years, my passion for them and for their salvation and freedom has only grown.

The more we acknowledge what the Lord has done, the more we see the impact that we have had. Remember, it is about your discipline and desire to tarry with the Lord. Leave the results up to God to answer in His timing, which may not be in your lifetime.

UNLIMITED

Andrew Murray exhorted us, "Beware in your prayers, above everything else, of limiting God, not only by unbelief, but by fancying that you know what He can do. Expect unexpected things 'above all that we ask or think.'"

When we pray but don't see immediate answers, it's easy for unbelief to enter and for the devil to challenge our faith. If he can convince us not to expect great things, he can get us to question our effectiveness and even God's ability. Ephesians 3:20–21 offers us assurance: "Now to Him who is able to do exceedingly abundantly above all that we ask or think, according to the power that works in us, to Him be glory in the church by Christ Jesus to all generations, forever and ever."

What can you ask of God that He cannot accomplish? What plan can you conceive that is beyond His ability to perform? When you doubt, remember that our God is able. When you don't see His hand moving, remember that *He is able*. He can accomplish anything, and nothing is beyond His power.

If God is for us and He is able, what do we have to lose? If we can train in prayer to tear down strongholds in people's lives and have an impact, why wouldn't we? If we know that life is short and that we're not guaranteed tomorrow, why wouldn't we spend our time making a difference in people's lives throughout the world? If we really believe these things, we will rise up in prayer.

The goal is to finish the race well, to get to end of our lives, face Jesus, and hear Him say, "Well done! You did all that you could do! You 'fought the good fight!' You prevailed in prayer! You made an impact! Well done!"

CHAPTER NINE

PREPARING FOR BATTLE

JOHN BORNSCHEIN

Have you ever read about the mighty men of King David (1 Chr 12:8–14)? These men were of great valor and physical strength. The Knights of the Round Table had nothing on them. First Chronicles 12:22 describes, "For day by day men came to David to help him, until there was a great army like the army of God" (NASB). Jashobeam killed 300 men with his spear in one battle (1 Chr 11:11–25), and Abishai struck down hundreds as well (2 Sam 23:18).

My favorite of these mighty men is Eleazar (2 Sam 23:9–10). While the armies fled from the Philistines, he stood his ground and brought down so many men that his hand froze to the sword. Eleazar had such courage that the armies of Israel were rallied and returned to defeat the enemy. Talk about faith and courage under fire! The enemy was strong. They were outnumbered and being defeated, but it took just one to stand firm and hold the line. He didn't do it alone; God was with him. But Eleazar had to be willing to allow God to work through him, to serve as an instrument or an extension of God's own hand. Eleazar had to take that first step, and the Almighty empowered him to do the rest.

I trained in the martial arts for years. Recently, I became a student in the combat style known as Jujitsu. When competing with weapons, we would engage in a tournament known as "king of the hill." The objective was to own the ring by battling each person who entered one at a time until you yourself were defeated. This would often occur after the "king" was utterly exhausted. The interesting thing is that no matter how well you conditioned, this would not take very long.

I remember defeating three well-rested men in the ring. I took a beating, but I was respected for standing my ground against three trained combatants. When I read the verses of the mighty men of David for the first time, I was literally in awe. It seemed unfathomable that a man could physically overcome 300 men. These weren't just farmers either—we're taking 300 *warriors*. Only God could grant that kind of physical strength to any human being. (This was not uncommon; Samson was granted that power as well.)

War is waged in several forms. God would often send Israel into battle, frequently executing His judgment where required. Since Adam, there have been more than 14 thousand recorded wars and 14 billion deaths.[1] In 5,603 years, there are only 292 years of time recorded without a major battle taking place.[2] This means that there are 5,311 years of documented physical combat for people. On the other hand, the spiritual battle began well before Adam was even given breath.

A WORLD IN WAR

Revelation declares, "Woe to the earth and the sea, because the devil has come down to you, having great wrath, knowing that he has only a short time" (Rev 12:12 NASB). In this "short time," there will always be war (Ezek 7:25). There is only one peace and only one hope—Jesus Christ, our Lord and King. As Ephesians 2:14 states, "For He Himself is our peace, who made both groups into one and broke down the barrier of the dividing wall" (NASB).

If you are in Christ, you are a new creation—a child of the King. But being a Christian, a follower of Christ, does not guarantee you peace on earth; you are also an enemy of the one who roams this world. As Jesus said in Matthew 10:34, "Do not think that I came to bring peace on the earth; I did not come to bring peace, but a sword" (NASB). Trouble and trials will come because our hope in Christ is for salvation and a renewed life in the new kingdom (Heb 13:14). Only there—in the new kingdom—will be our true peace. For now, we are tested and tried to be made unto His likeness. Thus, we must prepare for battle—it will come whether we are ready or not. This battle requires training in the physical and the spiritual. Through our struggle, our combat, we are shaped and conformed like iron sharpening iron. In this, the faithful will emerge.

We must put on the armor that our general has given to us and train as diligent soldiers. The first step is to pray—to be on our knees before the King. When a soldier is in prayer, this is sacred and holy ground (Exod 3:5), for where God is, the enemy cannot be. Soldiers must read the Scripture as though they were training with a sword. A knight couldn't pick up a sword at birth and overcome an adversary; likewise, a Christian who is unskilled with the word of God could not defeat an enemy or save a life.

David did not go to battle without first petitioning the Lord— asking Him for permission to engage and for favor in battle and victory (1 Sam 30:1–19). But how often do we rush to start our day without first going to God in prayer? How often do we lay out our plans and then seek God's counsel and wisdom? Prayer should be our first engagement, not our last response.

KNOWING THE ENEMY

In his first letter to the people of Corinth, Paul writes,

> Do you not know that in a race all the runners run, but only one gets the prize? Run in such a way as to get the prize. Everyone who competes in the games goes into strict training. They do it to get a crown that will not last, but we do it to get a crown that will last forever. Therefore I do not run like someone running aimlessly; I do not

fight like a boxer beating the air. No, I strike a blow to my body and make it my slave so that after I have preached to others, I myself will not be disqualified for the prize. (1 Cor 9:24–27)

When I first read these words, I was challenged to understand the context in which Paul was speaking. You see, the boxers he was referring to used gloves made of metal and leather straps rather than the boxing gloves we are familiar with today. Thus when he says that he "beats" his body, this is not something to take lightly. He was faced with the same temptations we struggle with today. His response was not to shun the enemy but to recognize his own weakness and respond with training and determination. We should apply this diligently in our lives as well. A strong, properly focused will coupled with the Holy Spirit is a powerful combination.

When you are doing God's will, you can expect opposition. When David was called to be the next king of Israel, he was pursued by Saul, and many people wanted to kill him. When Nehemiah was called to rebuild the walls of Jerusalem, he faced many challenges as well. As any warrior knows, it's vital to know who your enemy is so you can understand how to defeat him. Peter offers us this warning about our enemy: "Be alert and of sober mind. Your enemy the devil prowls around like a roaring lion looking for someone to devour (1 Pet 5:8–9).

Our enemy takes his battle very seriously, and he is out to destroy us and take our crowns. Here are some other characteristics of our adversary:

- He is subtle and wily.
- The devil is spiritual. (Not everything spiritual is righteous.)
- If you are marked by God, the devil has no power over you. You are impervious to death until your mission is complete.
- He can only inflict permissible wounds.
- His primary weapons are deceit and temptation.

ALL OR NOTHING

Psalm 116:15 states, "Precious in the sight of the Lord is the death of his saints." Why? Death is only a passage from one life to the next; the deceased saints gave their lives because they were dedicated to a greater purpose. In his essay, "Christian Behavior," C.S. Lewis writes, "If you read history you will find that the Christians who did most for the present world were precisely those who thought most of the next. It is since Christians have largely ceased to think of the other world that they have become so ineffective in this."[3] The sacrifice of the temporal for the eternal is what separates the wheat from the chaff (Matt 3). There is no room for lukewarm believers in God's kingdom. As Revelation 3:16 states, "Because you are lukewarm, and neither hot nor cold, I will spit you out of My mouth" (NASB).

God doesn't want our sloppy seconds; it is all or nothing. In his book, *Crazy Love*, Francis Chan illustrates what this means:

> When I was in high school, I seriously considered joining the Marines; this was when they first came out with the commercials for "the few, the proud, the Marines." But you know what? I didn't bother to ask if they would modify the rules for me so I could run less, and maybe also do fewer push-ups. That would've been pointless and stupid, and I knew it. Everyone knows that if you sign up for the Marines, you have to do whatever they tell you. They own you. Somehow this realization does not cross over to our thinking about the Christian life. Jesus didn't say that if you wanted to follow Him you could do it in a lukewarm manner. He said, "Take up your cross and follow me."[4]

Either you're a warrior for the Lord or you're not. Make the commitment right now that you are going to lay down your life for the Lord, taking up the cross and following Him.

Christ was confronted with people who were too comfortable with their lives, and He challenged them. He told a son to leave his family and follow Him (Matt 8:21–22). He told a wealthy man that to follow Him would mean total sacrifice, stressing that even the Son of Man didn't have a pillow to lay His head upon (Matt 8:18–20). He told another that he should sell all that he had and give to the poor (Matt 19:16–30). In each case, these eager men were cut to their heart because they wanted to be good but not great. They weren't willing to go all the way. But Jesus promises a reward for full commitment: "And everyone who has left houses or brothers or sisters or father or mother or wife or children or fields for my sake will receive a hundred times as much and will inherit eternal life" (Matt 19:29–30).

When the heat turns up in this society—and it most certainly will—are you going to be willing to walk into the furnace for your faith or step into the lion's den? Will you be willing to give it all for Him? The Holy Spirit will give you strength when that moment comes (Acts 7:54–60), but *you* must take the first step.

FACING A DEFEATED ENEMY

Adrian Rogers said, "Satan's real war is not with you … it is with God. Evil persons have always known that if they cannot harm someone directly, harm someone that they love and you've hurt them. Satan's war is with God, but he has set his attack on you because God has set His affection on you."[5] Satan wants you in a constant state of turmoil, a constant state of fear. He wants you to focus on your growing time constraints, the pending layoff or financial pressures, illnesses, and other distractions because he wants you to begin to doubt God's provision, God's promises, and God's love for you.

Paul tells us how we may live victoriously in this present evil age in spite of satanic opposition: we live victoriously through God's ability and the power of His might. In John 17:15, Jesus prayed to the Father, "My prayer is not that you take them out of the world but that you protect them from the evil one." It's important that we don't underestimate Satan, but it's just as important that we don't *overestimate* his power either. You and I face a defeated enemy. Jesus paid the price; He destroyed and annihilated the works of the devil. Now you can face all your battles with the armies of heaven at your side. It's like a mopping up operation in which the war has already been won and there remain only a few battles.

What feeds the spirit is that which drives the mind and directs the body. Read the following verse: "And now, compelled by the Spirit, I am going to Jerusalem, not knowing what will happen to me there. I only know that in every city the Holy Spirit warns me that prison and hardships are facing me. However, I consider my life worth nothing to me; my only aim is to finish the race and complete the task the Lord Jesus has given me—the task of testifying to the good news of God's grace" (Acts 20:22–24). Paul was so dedicated to kingdom work that he was no longer deterred by physical abuse. He was on a mission.

In the book of Acts, Paul knows the enemy lies ahead and will surely harm him for speaking truth. But does he turn back and run? No. He perseveres knowing that cuts, bruises, and broken bones are no obstacle for truth. And he counts these hardships all joy, for the greater good of the ministry to which he was called. That is passion—taking up a cross and modeling the one who gave it all.

ENDNOTES

1. 14,000 wars/14 billion deaths: Dr. Victor Yagodinsky, M.D.; http://english. pravda.ru/science/mysteries/06-10-2009/109689-criminal-0; http://www.bronx. com/news/world/553.html.

2. War (Collateral Damage): Wanted: Winning Warriors (March, 2003 POL), http://www.crosswalk.com/pastors/11545456/; J. K. Laney, *Marching Orders*, 50ff.

3. C.S. Lewis, "Christian Behavior."

4. Francis Chan, *Crazy Love* (Colorado Springs: David C. Cook, 2008), 80.

5. Adrian Rogers, *The Full Armor of God*. Tape. Accessed August 18, 2008.

CHAPTER TEN

THE WHOLE ARMOR OF GOD

JOHN BORNSCHEIN AND BRIAN TOON

Every day, as we pull out of the driveway, my family puts on armor, piece by piece. One of us will lead, saying, "And we put of the helmet of … salvation!" It isn't just any armor that we put on, it's the armor of God that Paul instructs his readers to put on in Ephesians 6:13–18,

> Take up the full armor of God, so that you will be able to resist in the evil day, and having done everything, to stand firm. Stand firm therefore, having *girded your loins with truth*, and having put on the *breastplate of righteousness*, and having shod your *feet* with the *preparation of the gospel of peace*; in addition to all, taking up the *shield of faith* with which you will be able to extinguish all the flaming arrows of the evil *one*. And take *the helmet of salvation*, and the *sword of the Spirit*, which is the *word of God*. With all prayer and petition *pray* at all times in the Spirit, and with this in view, be on the alert with all perseverance and petition for all the saints. (NASB, emphasis added)

Verbalizing each step is a great way to remind us of God's promise of our protection. God didn't just provide us with armor, He gave us *His* armor. Certainly God's armor is more than sufficient if we will just wear it and let it work—everyday. But we need the *whole* armor; missing just one piece leaves us vulnerable.

THE BELT OF TRUTH

In the New Testament era, men wore robes or gowns. When they fought or ran, they had to tuck their robes into their girdles, or what we would call a belt. The belt of truth allows us to fight without being entangled in our garments. Those who do not surround themselves with truth will become entangled in their own web of deceit and will fall.

Centuries ago, men would wrestle with only a belt because it was the first and preparatory piece of armor that a soldier wore. The object of the match was to remove the opponent's belt. If Satan can disarm us of our belt of truth, he can defeat us; deceit and lies are his greatest weapons. If we are under his control, it is because we have believed one of his lies instead of the truth of God's word. Jesus said, "I am … the truth" (John 14:6). To wear the belt of truth is to look toward Jesus to lead the way, to have your eyes singled only on Him.

THE BREASTPLATE OF RIGHTEOUSNESS

The word "righteousness" means a "pure life." Satan attacks with impurity, trying to break through the plates of the armor. We need to be aware of sin and to deal with it ruthlessly when it first presents itself, before it fully penetrates our breastplate.

Scripture mentions two basic kinds of righteousness. First is man's righteousness, which is the righteousness that people attempt to accomplish and perform without Christ. Isaiah tells us that all "our righteousnesses" are as filthy rags (Isa 64:6). This self-righteousness has no value to God. The second type of righteousness is God's own righteousness, which is imputed to us at salvation. God's righteousness comes only through faith; it is a gift and appropriated through Christ. Righteousness gives us total acceptance with God through Jesus.

Isaiah 59:17 specifically mentions the Messiah wearing the helmet of salvation and the breastplate of righteousness. With that breastplate, Jesus faced every temptation of Satan with 100 percent victory. He was 100 percent obedient to the Father, and He was "without blemish and without spot" (1 Pet 1:19 NKJV). Now, God has given us that same breastplate to us so that we, too, can live a holy and undefiled life. The moment you received Christ by faith, you were cleansed of all sin and clothed in Christ's breastplate of righteousness. Through Christ, you have power over sin; you are no longer controlled by your sinful nature but by His Spirit within you. That breastplate stands against lust, greed, envy, and jealously. But we must be steadfast to resist temptation.

We often think that the outward expression of anger will put a person in their place. But "the wrath of man does not produce the righteousness of God" (Jas 1:20 NKJV). Anger against another person makes us play right into the hand of the devil. The way to overcome the spiritual powers that come against us through individuals is to turn the other cheek (Matt 5:39) and take the issue up in prayer.

FEET SHOD WITH THE GOSPEL OF PEACE

These military shoes (which are similar to football cleats) not only allowed soldiers to move rapidly, but they also gave them stability in hand-to-hand combat. In the spiritual realm, the shoes of the gospel of peace make a messenger prepared to share the glad tidings of peace.

Life often brings obstacles, slippery slopes, and discouragement that attempts to make you lose your footing and stumble. Do you have the peace of God to enable you to walk through any difficulty? For me, whenever discouraging thoughts arise, my peace comes from reminding myself of how God has provided for me in the past while reciting Bible verses that promise prosperity and peace.

THE SHIELD OF FAITH

Faith comes from God, who squelches all of Satan's fiery darts. We need to constantly inspect and reinforce this shield of faith by reminding ourselves of all of the times the Lord has achieved victory. Ephesians 6:16 teaches us that our shield of faith will quench *all* the fiery darts of the wicked. Once a person starts standing on the word of God, the attack intensifies (2 Tim 3:12; Mark 4:17). But victory over all the attacks of the enemy is possible.

Paul said, "Now thanks be to God who always leads us in triumph in Christ" (2 Cor 2:14 NKJV). Teaching that God wills us to fail at times is like telling an athlete that his coach wants him to lose. We all learn from defeats and experiencing a loss can refine us, but real winners never plan to lose. Christians who plan to lose *will* lose.

THE HELMET OF SALVATION

The helmet is a constant reminder of the deliverance that God gives us; we have won the war in the end against Satan. What the helmet was to the Roman soldier, salvation is to the Christian soldier. There can be no victory unless the mind is protected with God's word.

Romans 8:6 says, "For to be carnally minded is death, but to be spiritually minded is life and peace" (NKJV). A significant battlefield for Christians is in the area of our minds. We must be careful to protect ourselves from wrong or improper thought patterns and be transformed by the renewing of our minds (Rom 12:2). Every thought can be brought captive to the obedience of Jesus Christ (2 Cor 10:4–5).

The Roman helmet also protected the jawbone, with armor extending down to the chin. We must control our tongues and speak words that glorify God (Eph 4:29; Jas 3:1–12), stating that we have overcome the darkness and that no weapon formed against us shall prosper.

THE SWORD OF THE SPIRIT

God doesn't mean for us to fight a defensive battle; He doesn't intend for us to just suit up in our armor and take blow after blow from the enemy without striking back. That's why He's given us the sword of His Spirit—His living word contained in the Bible.

It's not the Bible lying on your coffee table that makes the enemy flee, but the trained mind filled with the knowledge of truth, activated by the power of the Holy Spirit and exercised in an appropriate situation. It's similar to what Jesus said in the Gospel of John: "the words that I speak unto you, they are spirit and they are life" (John 6:63 KJV).

The sword is only useful if you keep it sharp. Keep your knowledge of God's word sharp by constantly reading it, meditating on it, and speaking His promises. Satan loves to keep us out of the word. To make Scripture reading and meditation a priority, we need to think of it as more important than food or sleep. Then, it will take on a whole new perspective.

FIGHT THE GOOD FIGHT

In one of his letters, Paul encouraged Timothy to "fight well in the Lord's battles" (1 Tim 1:18 NLV). The incredible thing to remember is that we are not alone in this battle. We need only to ask for the courage and God will be with us. In 2 Kings 6:17, when Elisha asked God to "open his eyes that he may see," God "opened the servant's eyes and he saw; and behold, the mountain was full of horses and chariots of fire all around Elisha" (2 Kgs 6:17 NASB). Just like Elisha, we, also, can go bearing the seal of the most high and we will never, ever be alone.

Judges 6–8 offers the incredible story of Gideon, who God chose to lead a band of only 300 men against thousands. God appointed an unqualified military leader and stripped him of soldiers, thinning out their numbers and selecting only the ones who would give it all for Him. Then He told them to put their weapons away. What kind of general does that? But that is exactly how God works. God didn't reveal His plan until the men had fully committed to go where He led. When God acts, He explodes boundaries and forces us to go where we aren't comfortable, and then He does a work that is awesome and unbelievable. Just as the Father drove the enemy into submission before Gideon, He will break down strongholds through you. Here are some important points to remember:

- **Armor is essential to our survival as Christian soldiers, but we are not invincible**. We are on our knees always. Only God grants victory, and sometimes He allows injury to stimulate growth for the greater good.
- **We must function as a unit.** If one person is weak and undisciplined, he or she can pull the whole army down. We must take courage and be strong, supporting one another and doing our part to fortify the unit. As Hebrews 10:24–25 states, "Let us consider how to stimulate one another to love and good deeds, not forsaking our own assembling together, as is a habit of some, but encouraging one another" (NASB). There is strength in numbers; we need to value the soldier who is with us.
- **Take the enemy seriously.** We need to take our purpose in life seriously. We are not here to be self-serving. We have a mission to do, so let's get to it.

When we put on the full armor of God, we are only positioning ourselves for battle; we then need to take the field of battle in prayer. Prayer is not just what we do before the battle; frequently, it *is* the battle. Prayer is what accomplishes results. This is evident in Exodus 17, when Moses stood on a hill overlooking Joshua and the Israelite army engaged in battle with the Amalekites. As Moses stood firm, rod in hand, he prayed over the battle. When his arms, raised in prayer, grew weary and fell, the tide turned against Joshua and his army. But when his arms were lifted high, they began to overcome and victory was at hand. The soldiers fought the Amalekites in the valley below, and on the hill above, Moses waged battle in prayer.

When Moses' arms grew tired, he sat on a stone while Aaron and Hur held his hands up—one on each side. In that way, his hands remained steady till sunset, and Joshua was victorious. His prayer won the battle in conjunction with what was done in the natural. Leaders must cover those on the front line in intercession before the Father, and it is critical that we do our part to be available and provide physical aid whenever and wherever it is necessary to do the Lord's work. This mission is a tandem effort as we engage the enemy on all fronts.

PRAYER WINS

In Matthew 21:21–22, Jesus encouraged His disciples with these words: "Truly I say to you, if you have faith, and do not doubt, you will not only do what was done to the fig tree, but even if you say to this mountain, 'Be taken up and cast into the sea,' it shall happen. And all things you ask in prayer, believing, you shall receive" (NASB). Prayer is another form of absolute dependence and reliance upon God for His divine intervention. Remember these points:

- **There is a right way and a wrong way to pray.** Fortunately, God is patient and looks to the heart. Remember, you are no stronger than your prayer life.
- **Prayer is communion with God**—fellowship, relationship, and intimacy with Him. The devil wants to keep us from praying. He mocks our schemes and laughs at our toiling, but he also fears our prayers.
- **Asking is *one* aspect of prayer, but it is not *the* purpose of prayer**. The purpose of God granting requests is that the Father would be glorified through the name of His Son.
- **Prayer is conversation**; it is dialogue, not monologue. It's not just petitioning God with two choices: "God, please do A or B." We must ask Him for what He wants, too, and then

be prepared to submit to His will. We need to meditate on His word, and then "Be still and know that [He is] God" (Psa 46:10).

- **Prayer builds perception.** Are you blessed or stressed? When you magnify God, you realize just how insignificant your problems really are. Praise Him for the blessings you have rather than just bombarding Him with perceptions of what you lack. If you are caving into stress, step up your prayer life and Scripture reading in proportion to the intensity of the attack.

It's easy to get caught up in the delights of this world, but we need to try hard not to lay up treasures here. When we read James 4:13–15, which says that we are a vapor, it is easy to realize our place. Ecclesiastes 5:15 serves as another reminder of this: "As he [the rich man] had come naked from his mother's womb, so will he return as he came. He will take nothing from the fruit of his labor that he can carry in his hand" (NASB). The Father implores us to avoid the desires of our sin nature: "What good will it be for someone to gain the whole world, yet forfeit their soul? Or what can anyone give in exchange for their soul?" (Matt 16:26). We belong to the Lord and every day is a gift.

As culture continues to crumble by casting out truth for moral relativism (godlessness and lawlessness), we must realize that the Church is a stronghold in this world. We are lifting the standard on the battlefield, and we must stand firm. Remember the words of Deuteronomy 20:3–4, "Today you are going into battle against your enemies. Do not be fainthearted or afraid, panic or be terrified by them. For the LORD your God is the one who goes with you to fight for you against your enemies to give you victory." We must be confident that the Lord will grant us victory (Prov 21:31).

CHAPTER ELEVEN

THE WEAPONS OF OUR WARFARE

DAVID BUTTS

One of the key reasons for prayerlessness in the Christian life is a theological one. Deep inside, many Christians believe that prayer really doesn't matter; God is going to do whatever He is going to do, and prayer isn't really going to change anything. If that is so, then why pray? Why spend time doing that which is ineffective for change? S.D. Gordon provides us with an answer: "The purpose of prayer is not to persuade or influence God, but to join forces with him against the enemy."[1]

The Bible teaches that prayer not only changes the person who prays, it also changes situations. Scripture is filled with examples of people whose situations changed as a result of their prayer—whether on a personal scale, such as a Hannah praying for a son (1 Sam 1:9–18), or on a national scale, such as King Jehoshaphat praying for deliverance for Judah (1 Chr 20:1–23).

STANDING IN THE GAP

One of the best teachings on the power of prayer comes from Ezekiel 22:30: "I looked for someone among them who would build up the wall and stand before me in the gap on behalf of the land so I would not have to destroy it, but I found no one." This verse shows us the all-powerful Creator of the universe looking for someone to pray before He begins to act. The people of God had sinned and rebelled against Him and faced the punishment for their disobedience; in this case, the punishment was the destruction of the city of Jerusalem. But our merciful God was willing to delay or even avert this catastrophe if someone would intercede before Him on Jerusalem's behalf—if someone would "stand in the gap." God looked for such a person, but could find no one. Prayer could have made a difference then, and it still can today. God is waiting for His people to "stand before Him" on behalf of our land (2 Chr 7:14).

The story of the Moses praying on the hill while the Israelites fought the Amalekites (Exod 17:10–13) that we discussed earlier also demonstrates how prayer changes things: "As long as Moses held up his hands, the Israelites were winning, but whenever he lowered his hands, the Amalekites were winning" (Exod 17:11). Why would the position of an old man's hands have anything to do with the battle in the valley below? Lifted hands have always been a symbol of prayer. As long as God was involved through prayer, Israel won. In Exodus 17:16, after the battle, Moses built an altar to the Lord and said, "Because hands were lifted up against the throne of the LORD." Moses' lifting his hands wasn't just idle spiritual calisthenics; it was an expression of the power of prayer to change situations.

HIT OR MISS

Why did Jesus pray? Was it simply to change Himself? Or did Jesus know that prayer was the way His Father had chosen to work on this planet? Jesus didn't waste time doing things just for religious show. Jesus prayed because prayer was His way of staying in touch with His Father and it demonstrated His dependency upon His Father. When Jesus prayed, He *expected* God to act. His great High Priestly prayer in John 17 demonstrated that He expected the Father to do things in response, both in His prayers as well as the prayers of His disciples.

Another one of the main reasons why so many Christians fail to pray or believe the wrong things about prayer is the seeming "hit or miss" aspect to much of our praying—sometimes it works, sometimes it doesn't. So we develop a bad theology to cover our misses and turn prayer into something it was never meant to be.

This problem happens when we look at prayer as a way of getting things from God. If we pray long enough, have enough faith, and get enough people to join us in prayer, maybe we'll get what we want from God. But prayer is not "our way of getting things from God"; prayer is God's chosen way of accomplishing His will on this planet. Our job in prayer is to draw near in intimacy. As we begin to understand a bit of the Lord's heart on a matter, then we begin to ask Him to accomplish what is already His will. It is at that point that prayer becomes a powerful change agent to achieve the Lord's purposes.

In spiritual warfare, it is prayer that keeps us connected to our commander-in-chief. Consequently, prayer becomes strategic in warfare. It is prayer that gives us our supply line of provisions for the battle. It is prayer that unleashes the power of God's word to accomplish its purpose in overcoming the enemy. John Piper said it this way: "Until you know that life is war, we won't know what prayer is for."[2]

WEAPONS OF WARFARE

In a sermon, Charles H. Spurgeon preached,

> Like the Spartans, every Christian is born a warrior. It is his destiny to be assaulted, his duty to attack. Part of his life will be occupied with defensive warfare. He will have to defend the *faith once delivered to the saints*. He will have to resist the devil. He will have to *stand against all the devil's wiles, and having done all, still to stand.* He will, however, be an ineffective Christian, if he acts only on the defensive. He must be one who goes against his foes, as well as [one who] stands still to receive their advance.

He must be able to say with David, "I come to thee in
the Name of the Lord of Hosts. The God of the armies of
Israel, whom thou has defied" (1 Sam 17:45).

The weapons we fight with are not the weapons of
the world. On the contrary: they have divine power to
demolish strongholds (2 Cor 10:4).[3]

We are in a war like no other. Because it is spiritual warfare,
the weapons that we use cannot be the normal weapons of this
world. The devil does not succumb to guns or bombs. Nor does he
surrender to human wisdom or strategies; to fight the devil, we need
spiritual weapons.

Jesus offered an example of spiritual weapons in use when He
resisted the devil in the wilderness. Whenever the devil tried to tempt
Him, Jesus replied by quoting from Scripture (e.g., Matt 4:1–11). With
every thrust of Satan's sword of lies, Jesus parried with the sword of
the Lord—God's word. Even the Son of God did not leave spiritual
warfare to His own strength of character or will; He instead fought
the battle with the spiritual weapon of the word of God. Jesus offers a
model for us to follow in our daily battle; we should know the word
of God so well that when we are asked our opinion on anything, we
naturally give God's.

On a very practical level, we can win this spiritual battle by using
the word of God and prayer. Prayer keeps us in communication with
our commander-in-chief. As we pray, He directs us, guides us, protects
us, and even shows us the parts of His word that are needed for the
victory at any given moment. Have you ever experienced the Spirit
working as His word comes to your mind at just the right time, for just
the right purpose?

PREVENTING CASUALTIES

As children, we would have what we called "sword drills" in our church
youth group. In contest form, we would try to respond to questions

our leaders asked us with the correct Bible verse as quickly as possible. Though we saw it as a game, we were being trained for a very real war. The soldier who must learn to use a weapon in the midst of battle is an unfortunate one. How much better it is to be trained in the proper use of your weapon in the safety and security of a training camp with your comrades?

When Paul admonishes Timothy to "Do your best to present yourself to God as one approved, a workman who does not need to be ashamed and who correctly handles the word of truth" (2 Tim 2:15), he is clearly calling Timothy to engage in serious training in the use of the spiritual weapon of the word. If we do not have a working knowledge of Scripture, we will likely become a casualty in this spiritual battle we are in. Remember, the best defense to warding off the attacks of the tempter is a good offense. And there is just no better offense against temptation than proper knowledge and use of the word of God.[4]

Most Christians agree that studying and knowing God's word is valuable. But we often fail when it comes to actually using the word in warfare. This is where prayer comes in. We must learn to pray God's word back to Him. Beth Moore explains this well in her book, *Praying God's Word*:

> In Ephesians 6:10–18, Paul listed the whole armor of God. Only one piece of the armor is actually a weapon. ... The sword of the Spirit, clearly identified as the Word of God. Is the only offensive weapon listed in the whole armor of God. Second Corinthians 10:3 uses the plural, assuring us we have weapons for warfare. What would the other primary weapon be? Perhaps additional weapons might be identified elsewhere, but I believe the other primary weapon of our warfare is stated right after the words identifying the sword of the Spirit as the Word of God in Ephesians 6:17. The next verse says, "And pray in the Spirit on all occasions." I am utterly convinced that the

two major weapons with divine power in our warfare are the Word of God and Spirit-empowered prayer.[5]

My wife and I often share with churches that the one thing that has changed our individual prayer lives is learning to pray the Lord's word back to Him. My favorite way to pray is, "open eyes, open Bible." As I read through the Bible, I'm led again and again to pray about that which is clearly God's will. I find myself praying about things I had never considered praying about in ways I had never expected to pray.

All of us can do that; it doesn't require special training or aptitude. We simply open our Bibles and begin to pray about what we are reading. Sometimes it is a matter of asking the Lord to teach us, to give us understanding of His word. Other times there are clear ways of praying the word into our own lives or the lives of those around us.

When I travel to different churches, I am often asked to pray for local congregations. There are many beneficial ways that I could pray over a congregation. But what I love to pray is what I know God desires to bring about in that fellowship, so I often turn to Ephesians 3:14 and begin praying around the verse in my own words, personalizing and applying Scripture to a particular group:

I kneel before you in prayer Father, from whom our whole family in heaven and on earth derives our name. I pray that out of your glorious riches you might strengthen this church with power through your Spirit in their inner being, so that you, Lord Jesus, might dwell in their hearts through faith. I pray that the brothers and sisters here, being rooted and established in love, might have the power, together with all the saints, to grasp how wide and long and high and deep is your love, O Christ. And that they might know this love that surpasses knowledge—that they might be filled to the measure of all your fullness, Lord.

This sort of praying overcomes the enemy. It is not based on emotions or desires, but on the revealed truth of God's will in Scripture. It touches God's heart because it emerges from His heart.

It is scriptural praying that allows us to resist the enemy, much as Jesus did in the wilderness temptations. Peter writes in 1 Peter 5:8: "Be alert and of sober mind. Your enemy the devil prowls around like a roaring lion looking for someone to devour." In the previous chapter, he writes, "Therefore be alert and of sober mind so that you may pray" (1 Pet 4:7). In both verses, he commands believers to practice self-control. Self-control is needed if we are to pray with power and passion. And prayer is needed if we are to be successful in resisting the devil.

ENDNOTES

1. S.D. Gordon, *Quiet Talks in Prayer*.

2. John Piper, *Let the Nations be Glad!* (Grand Rapids: Baker Academic, 2003), 45.

3. Charles Spurgeon, "The Shield of Faith" (sermon, Metropolitan Tabernacle, Newington, October 27, 1861).

4. Greg Laurie, *The Great Compromise* (Word Publishing 1994), 62–63.

5. Beth Moore, *Praying God's Word* (Nashville: B&H Publishing Group, 2009), 5.

CHAPTER TWELVE

EVERYDAY COMBAT READINESS

DAVID BUTTS

I once returned from a Christian conference so excited about prayer that I determined I would get up early the next morning and spend a significant amount of time praying. When my alarm clock went off at 5:30 a.m. (yes, God is up then), I got up and prepared myself for prayer. But no sooner had I begun praying when I had this overpowering urge to wash my car. My mind began to be filled with images of my dirty car and the hectic schedule for the day ahead that wouldn't allow me to get it washed. It became so overwhelming that I found myself getting off my knees and getting ready to go wash my car.

Then a question came flooding into my mind: "When was the last time you had an overwhelming desire to wash your car at 5:30 in the morning?" The answer, of course, was, never. Then where did the thought originate to quit praying and go wash my car? That morning, I began to realize that God wanted me to pray, and I wanted to pray, but the devil wanted me to wash my car. It made the decision to stay and pray very simple. Awareness of the enemy's attack was a key to victory in my prayer time that day.

RECOGNIZING REALITY

In Ephesians 6:18, Paul writes, "Be alert and always keep on praying." Alertness is a critical area for victory in spiritual warfare that Christians often ignore, to their grave danger. Scripture contains many commands in this area: be alert, watch, be careful, and be on your guard. You might think the authors of Scripture believed we were in some sort of danger that required us to be constantly aware and alert. Yet so many of us wander through life totally unaware of the dangers that lurk on every side.

I believe that 90 percent of the battle in the area of spiritual warfare is simply being aware that a battle is going on in and around us. Look at this from the perspective of actual physical warfare. Can you imagine a group of soldiers in the midst of a battle forgetting where they are? Planes are flying overhead, cannons are firing, bullets are whizzing by, but they forget completely about the battle raging around them, pack a nice lunch, and take off across the landscape looking for a nice spot to picnic. Every now and then as they walk, one of them gets injured, occasionally one is killed, and they stop and ask, "How can such bad things happen to such good people?"

Do you recognize this question? What's your response to this group of lost soldiers? Would you accuse them of failing to comprehend reality? Yet we are the same as them when we wander through our days with no awareness of the spiritual battles around us.

THE GIFT OF AWARENESS

Ephesians 6 offers a wonderful gift for helping us walk in awareness: the armor of God (Eph 6:10–24). Growing up in the Church, I heard about the armor of God many times. We preached it, taught it, analyzed it, and dissected it. We did everything except what the Bible told us to do: put it on.

Many years ago, when I finally understood what to do with the armor, I began putting on the armor of God every morning. Since then, I've trained myself to put on the armor daily as I begin my shower. When the water hits me, it serves as a reminder to begin to pray and put on my spiritual protection for the day. The third verse of the old hymn, "Stand Up, Stand Up for Jesus," offers another reminder: "Put on the gospel armor, each piece put on with prayer."

When I put on God's armor daily, I am reminded that I am in a battle. Awareness floods into my soul that I am awaking to danger that day. But even more, there is the quiet assurance that I follow the commander-in-chief of the Lord's armies; He has provided both victory and protection for me in the midst of the day's struggles. He has loaned me His very own armor. So I pray with great joy, gratefully accepting and clothing myself with His armor. Alert to the battle, prepared through prayer, I move through the day's battles not with fear, but with confidence in my Lord's victory.

Putting on the armor is also becoming clothed with Christ. Do you realize that every part of the armor corresponds to an attribute of Jesus? When we put on the helmet of salvation, we realize that Jesus' very name means "God is my salvation." The breastplate of righteousness reminds us that Jesus has become our righteousness. The fact that Jesus is the truth is hammered home as we put on the belt of truth. The Prince of Peace Himself reminds us to fasten to our feet the readiness of the gospel of peace. As we take up the shield of faith, we remember the Scriptures that speak of Him as the shield that goes before us. Wielding the sword of the Lord, God's word becomes a natural, daily activity for those who follow the Living Word of God.

BE PREPARED

James gives us some wonderful steps for combat readiness in James 4:7–8: "Submit yourselves, then, to God. Resist the devil, and he will flee from you. Come near to God and he will come near to you. Wash your hands, you sinners, and purify your hearts, you double-minded."

This passage from James is boot camp for believers—basic training for those preparing for battle:

- **Submit to God.** There should be no outright rebellion against God in our lives that would give the devil a foothold.
- **Come near to God.** This is a prayer life focused on intimacy with the Lord. This life of intimacy is a place of protection in the midst of warfare.
- **Wash our hands and purify our hearts.** This call to holiness is essential if we are to stand victorious.

In the midst of submitting to God, drawing near to Him, and walking in holiness, we are able to resist the devil.

It is important to understand that we do not simply do these things once and then leave them behind. Warfare is constant. We are called to vigilance. Submission, intimacy, holiness, and resistance to the devil will need to be a part of every day's prayer life. Here are some further steps for practical preparation for everyday warfare that need to be a part of your daily prayers.

- **Pray for protection.** It is appropriate to ask the Lord for protection each day for ourselves, our family, and others for whom we may have responsibility. This involves both spiritual and physical protection. It is dangerous to assume we are protected. God is concerned with our protection, and He wants us to ask in dependence upon Him (Ezra 8:21–23; Job 1:10; Psa 91; John 17:12, 15).
- **Pray for discernment**. In the midst of daily life, it is vital that we understand what is of the enemy and what may simply be the circumstances of life. When Paul wrote that "we are not unaware of [Satan's] schemes" (2 Cor 2:11), he implied that we have the ability to discern the hand of the enemy in the midst of life's happenings. This is especially vital for a local church as they deal with individuals and circumstances that may be creating problems. "Lord, is this

the hand of our enemy at work?" may be a most appropriate prayer.

- **Pray for opened spiritual eyes.** Paul wrote in 2 Corinthians 4:4 that the God of this age has blinded the minds of unbelievers. One of our most important prayers should be for God to remove the blindfolds from the minds of those whom we may have the opportunity to reach with the gospel of Jesus Christ.

- **Pray for blessing.** We have the wonderful privilege of praying God's blessing upon those in need. Whether it is for those in your own family or those on the other side of the planet, the prayer of blessing is an attack of light versus darkness. It is a word of hope in the midst of despair.

- **Pray for spiritual leaders.** There is an all-out attack by the forces of hell against spiritual leaders. We need to be praying for our ministers every day, as well as other leaders in our churches.

- **Pray for revival**. There is nothing that Satan hates like revival. An awakened church is his worst fear. As we pray daily for a great awakening of the body of Christ, we are doing great damage to the kingdom of darkness. One of the great moves of God's Spirit today is in calling the Church to fervent prayer for revival.

- **Pray for completion of the task of world evangelism**. The advance of God's kingdom throughout the world continues as people from every tribe, tongue, and nation give their lives to Jesus. Our prayers must reflect and reinforce this great move of God against the forces of darkness.

CHAPTER THIRTEEN

WEAPONS TRAINING: APPLICATION OF PRAYER

KATHY BRANZELL

I received a bottle of fancy lotion as a gift one Christmas. I chuckled as I noticed that there were directions on the back label (who doesn't know how to apply lotion?), but I took a closer look anyway—maybe this special lotion had to be applied a certain way. The directions read, "Apply liberally, being careful to cover all of the areas wherever you need it most, to restore balance to your life." Really? This must be some amazing lotion if it can moisturize my skin *and* restore balance to my life. On second glance, though, I noticed that it did not promise to moisturize, just balance.

My life probably looks a lot like yours does: busy. Time just seems to fly, leaving me wishing every night that I had more time for my friends and family. I have many responsibilities that I am grateful for: a husband, children, a home, ministry, teaching, writing, prayer and Bible study time, serving on boards of directors and committees. I thank God for His gifts and the opportunities to use them, but 24 hours just never seem like enough.

Can you relate to this? Am I the only one who is out of balance? I imagine you are nodding right now, maybe even adding things you never seem to be able to get done to my list. (I bet you wish you knew the name of this lotion so it could restore balance to your life, too.) Friend, we both know that no matter how much of that lotion I squeezed out of that tube, it was *not* going to balance out this crazy life.

But I know something that does restore balance to my life. It cuts through the chaos and helps me to prioritize and make decisions. It must be applied daily, even several times per day, lavishly—especially in areas where I need it most. It is the application of prayer. As Christians, we may believe—just as I did with the lotion—that we don't need directions for prayer. But most of us do not really know how to *apply* prayer. We might know how to pray based on the example taught to us by our family or church service, but we will always have a capacity to grow in our understanding and ability to pray and apply the power of prayer.

Even some of the most amazing prayer warriors will tell you that they do not comprehend the vastness of the power, passion, and profit of praying to an all-powerful, all-loving God. He bends down from heaven to hear our prayers, delights in hearing from His children, desires and knows what is best for us, and is waiting for us to ask for His help. No man or woman can comprehend the full meaning and benefit of prayer. But wherever you are right now, whatever you know at this moment, you can to apply prayer. You can commit to pray like you're applying for help—as a request or as a person applies for aid or a job. And you can also commit to *apply prayer*—to achieve a result, to spread it thoroughly over your life, spending significant time and effort in the area of prayer so that you become relevant in all situations and circumstances.

APPLICATION

My formal compilation of the definitions and synonyms of the word "application" would look something like this: "The process of putting something into use diligently, with devotion and attention, therefore acknowledging its relevance and value in a specific area or for a specific task." My less formal explanation is this: "Prayer is our faithful response of action in every emotion, responsibility, relationship, or event in our lives."

Before we panic, cry, get angry, freak out, quit, blame, or feel guilty, anxious, or depressed, we pray. And then if we need to, we pray some more. Likewise, before we call a friend, celebrate, throw a party, or jump up and down, we pray (and then pray some more). The application of prayer includes praying in the joy-filled victory moments of life as well as the hard, bad-news days of life.

In Philippians 4:6, Paul writes, "Do not be anxious about anything, but in every situation, by prayer and petition, with thanksgiving, present your requests to God." He says something similar in Colossians 4:2: "Devote yourselves to prayer, being watchful and thankful." These verses direct us to the foundation of prayer application: faith.

We do not turn to prayer as one of many solutions; God is the solution. We pray in faith. And we are anxious about nothing; instead, we are thankful and faith-filled, that as 2 Timothy 1:12 says, "For this reason I also suffer these things, but I am not ashamed; for I know whom I have believed and I am convinced that He is able to guard what I have entrusted to Him until that day" (NASB).

The foundation of prayer application is to be convinced—to believe—that God is able and willing to do the very best thing in every matter that we entrust to Him in prayer. Proverbs 23:12 states, "Apply your heart to instruction and your ears to words of knowledge." It was not enough for me to just have my bottle of lotion; keeping it in a drawer in my nightstand was not going to help me in any way. Likewise, simply having knowledge about prayer, God, Scripture, or Christian history will not change your life; only applying this knowledge to your heart will make a significant difference.

Lessons One and Two:
Pray at all times, and believe at all times.

People apply lotion in many different ways. Some people squeeze the lotion onto one fingertip, and others use the palms of their hands.

Some people rub the lotion between both palms and then spread it on other parts of their body, but others put it directly on a specific area and then use their hands to massage it in. Likewise, there are many ways to apply prayer. Think about these two questions before you go any further:

- What do you know about God?
- What do you know about prayer?

Some people have been praying the same words or the same way all of their Christian lives, not realizing that there are many ways to apply prayer. If you grew up in a praying home, your first prayers were probably a blessing or grace at the meal table. For some of you, it may have been the same prayer, same words, at every meal. Others may have experienced conversation-like praying that was specific to the day's events, needs, and blessings. Both types of prayer, said with a loving heart, are absolutely pleasing to God; it is a pause to acknowledge His presence at the table and a thankfulness to Him as the provider of what you are about to eat.

A second prayer you were taught was probably at bedtime. Again, it may have been a memorized prayer that your repeated every night or a different prayer every night that included requests, thanks, and any other things you wanted to make sure God knew about. I love to listen to a child's prayers; they are so sweet and honest, full of love and assurance that God is not only real and really listening, but the faith that He will do something about it. The first lesson we can learn from a child is this: apply prayer immediately and in all situations. And the second lesson is this: know that God is real, really listening, and will do something about it. For this lesson, we can find support from Psalm 145:19, which states, "He fulfills the desires of those who fear him; he hears their cry and saves them" (NASB).

It is important to remember that His response may not be the response you were looking for. It may not come in the timing you wanted or the way you wanted. I have always appreciated the many examples of how God answers prayer in addition to the simple "yes" or "no":

- "Later"
- "With hard work and perseverance"
- "Not for you, but someone else"
- "My grace is sufficient"
- "It is not for you to understand. I will reveal what I decide to show you."
- "Trust and obey"
- "My ways are not your ways, nor My thoughts your thoughts"

It's not usually a simple yes or no answer. Life is complicated, but God is complete. Most of what we face in life we could never answer just "yes" or "no"; there might be an explanation, research, experience, or other priorities that we have to achieve or learn first. But rest assured: God is Omniscient and all-knowing. There is nothing that He does not know or has not seen; nothing escapes His attention. He does not get distracted, and no one can fool Him. He can even see beyond our actions and know the intensions of our heart. We, on the other hand, don't know many things.

Lesson Three:
God knows all things, and He will do the right thing about it.

I received a phone call from an acquaintance whose child attended the same school as my daughter. She was furious and suspicious of our principal because he had been hard to contact and had not returned her calls, as he had been absent from school recently. As I listened to her vent, I was careful not to reveal any information that I had been told in confidence by my close friend, the principal.

"I have always liked and respected him, but this is unforgivable," She said. "He must not care about my daughter or the school anymore, since he was off interviewing for other jobs at other schools."

I asked her, "Do you know for sure he is interviewing at other schools?"

"Well, no," she replied, "but—"

I cut her off before she could continue. "Have you talked with him personally about your concerns?"

"Of course not. I told you I can't get ahold of him. But when I do, he'll be sorry he ever ignored my calls."

Knowing where the principal was and the personal tragedy that was going on in his life, I calmly asked, "Knowing his integrity and heart, could there be something that you don't know—a good reason that has nothing to do with interviews, or avoiding you, that is the reason behind all this?"

There was a long pause and then another question. "Why, what do you know?"

"I'm asking you to give him a piece of your heart instead of a piece of your mind right now," I answered. "I'm not at liberty to say what he has confided in me, but I would ask you to pray for him instead of condemning him."

A couple of weeks later, the principal shared with the staff and parents about his battle with cancer, and three days later, the newspaper reported the unexpected death of his son.

How tragic it would have been for this woman to heap coals of anger and accusation on this man who had just been diagnosed with cancer and was struggling over losing his son? How would she have felt then? How about you? Have you ever judged someone only to find out later that you were completely wrong? Have you ever spewed your hurt, disappointment, or anger at someone, only to regret every word of it? Have you ever said, "If I knew then what I know now"?

In Jeremiah 29:11–13, the Lord says, "For I know the plans that I have for you … plans for welfare and not for calamity to give you a future and a hope. Then you will call upon Me and come and pray to Me, and I will listen to you. You will seek Me and find Me when you search for Me with all your heart" (NASB). In situations where something is just not right but you don't know what it is, talk to God about it. When a friend is not acting like herself or you encounter gossip or speculation, talk to God. Tell God what you saw, felt, or heard, and then ask for His wisdom. Ask Him to show you where you can help. Ask Him to silence the gossip. Ask Him to supply whatever that person or situation needs.

If you feel that you are a victim of harshness, neglect, or hurt, tell God about the situation and pour out your feelings to Him. King David wrote great examples of this in the Psalms. He often starts a psalm complaining—even tattling—to God about his enemies, woes, hurt feelings, and suffering. But by the end of the psalm, he is rejoicing in God's goodness and remembering His faithfulness and blessing.

Talking to God in prayer will keep you from feeling the need to go talk to other people. They, like my lotion, may promise to help you, but they do not have any real authority, insight, or power. Compulsion, corruption, and consumption are never the right response—in fact, they may make matters worse. Like my lotion bottle, these things make you believe that they can do something that is totally out of the realm of their ability. But they will not resolve the conflict you have with another person any more than that lotion will balance my life. God, on the other hand, can.

In times of trouble, we must face conflicts head on with prayer; we must apply prayer liberally to restore the balance to our emotions, actions, and decisions. And we must remember this: God is real; He is really listening, and not only will He do something about it, but He, knowing all things, will do the right thing about it.

Lesson Four:
Prayer gives us access to one who is immeasurably more than anyone we could ever reach for here on earth.

In times of struggle, we learn that prayer is our first, immediate response. It is not what we come to after we are all out of ideas or have tapped out our resources. If prayer comes first, we will not be at the end of anything. Prayer is the beginning of peace and resolution; it is reaching for joy. It puts feet to our faith, and it protects us from dumb decisions and regretful reactions. Prayer is a response of relationship with the one and only God.

Second Samuel 22 records a prayer of King David. I return to this passage time and time again when I am feeling the enemy advancing in an area of my life that involves my family, ministry, friends, community, or nation. It is a reminder to me of the victory that comes from crying out to one who can do immeasurably more than anything or anyone else on this earth could ever do. David's prayer concludes with these words: "The LORD lives! Praise be to my Rock! Exalted be God, the Rock, my Savior! He is the God who avenges me, who puts the nations under me, who sets me free from my enemies. You exalted me above my foes; from a violent man you rescued me. Therefore I will praise you, LORD, among the nations; I will sing the praises of your name" (2 Sam 22:47–50).

We are never out of God's reach. As the saying goes, "Don't tell God how big your problem is, but rather, tell your problem, your enemy, your mountain, how big your God is!" Nothing can give you the guidance, joy, understanding, strength, compassion, comfort, patience, or resources that God can. No one can even come close.

Lesson Five:
Prayer is a respectful response to a relationship with God.

Matthew 6:8 states that our heavenly Father knows what we need before we even ask. This may lead you to question, "If God knows what I need and He loves me, why do I have to ask?" Remember this:

prayer is a respectful response to a relationship with God. And it gives us access to one who is immeasurably more than anything or anyone we could ever reach for here on earth.

Imagine this scenario: your son comes in from school very angry, giving you the cold shoulder and slamming cabinets in the kitchen while you are sitting at the table. Finally, he breaks the silence with this disrespectful question: "Why didn't you buy me a yearbook? Everyone else got their yearbooks today, but I did not get one."

You are startled by this behavior and reply, "When did you ask me to buy you a yearbook?"

He replies, "I shouldn't have to ask you. I get a yearbook every year. You know they sell them, and you should have gone up there and bought it when they were selling them."

You then ask, "How was I supposed to know when they were selling them if you didn't tell me or ask me for the money to buy it?"

Then he delivers the final blow: "You just should, that's what parents are supposed to do."

We can't wait around for God to shower us with blessings without so much as a humble, respectful conversation about the desires of our heart—a hurt that needs comfort, a decision that needs guidance, strength for a trial, courage to overcome a fear. Yes, God knows we need it, but we need to humble ourselves and ask. Otherwise, we are no different than the bratty child.

Remembering to say "thank you" is vital. Perhaps we haven't received what we are asking for now because we weren't grateful for the last blessing. This is another lesson on ways we pray: prayer is access to God, but we gain access for many different reasons. We may access God in order to praise Him for all that He is—for His unchanging attributes that makes Him the King of kings and Lord of lords. Or we may gain access in order to apologize, to confess our sins, to admit wrongdoings, and to seek forgiveness and cleansing. We also gain access for the sake of others, to take others to the throne of God in intercession. We pray heartfelt prayers, memorized or conversational, and we can tell God our hurt and concerns in a way that we are refraining from judgment and gossip, but simply going to the Father who knows all and has the authority to do the right thing.

But we should always remember to access God to thank Him for everything—for life and breath, for His creation and His love, for prayers answered "yes," and for His protection and wisdom when He answers "no." We must thank Him for family, food, our homes, education, jobs, transportation, communication, all of our opportunities, gifts, possessions, our church, relationships, our abilities. A respectful relationship realizes that access to someone does not mean you are constantly taking from them but never giving and never appreciative. I imagine that you would not be friends for long with someone who took, and took, and took from you but never gave so much as a "Thank you," much less anything else. That is not a relationship. As Galatians 4:6–7 says, "Because you are sons, God has sent forth the Spirit of His Son into our hearts, crying, 'Abba! Father!' Therefore you are no longer a slave, but a son; and if a son, then an heir through God" (NASB). God is our Father, we are His children and heirs (Rom 8:16). When we abide in Him, amazingly, He calls us friend.

Saying thank you has become one of the main aspects of my prayer life. I wake up and thank Him for another day of life and opportunities to know Him and make Him known. I lie down at night and thank Him for His covering through that day, for the people I saw, for a safe place to sleep. If you are ever short on things to pray over, just think through your day or turn on the news.

In stretching the idea of our "prayer life" as going beyond simply having a prayer time, we learn to pray beyond our urgent needs and pray in praise, confession, thanksgiving, intercession, and requests. These prayers may consist of one or two words; we may pray "wow!" at a sunset or "help me" at the sight of a temptation. Our prayers may be a song, a poem, or a speechless cry, or a sobbing groan. Entering into God's presence in prayer means bringing Him into your heart and mind. You are always already in His.

Lesson Six:
The humble prayers of the faithful always result in gain and glory.

Second Chronicles 7:14 offers an important lesson in prayer: "if my people … will humble themselves and pray and seek my face and turn from their wicked ways, then I will hear from heaven, and I will forgive their sin and will heal their land." The humble prayers of the faithful always result in gain and glory. Thankfully, God knows what we need and watches over us day and night; He never leaves us or forsakes us (Heb 13:5). When we approach God in prayer, we can always count on attaining something. God, in His wisdom, knows what we really need (not necessarily agreeing with what we want), and He is faithful to provide.

Like a good parent, God does not throw open the storehouses to spoil us rotten, but He enjoys rewarding us. He commands and rewards obedience, and He is satisfied when we listen to His guidance and follow it. He loves a cheerful giver, and He gives to those who are content with what they already have. He lifts up the lowly and brings down the proud; He disciplines those He loves. We may not receive that for which we came, but what He gives is better gain.

In John 15, Jesus teaches us that we cannot bear good fruit if we do not abide in Him, and that apart from Him we can do nothing (John 15:4–5). In John 15:7–8, He says, "If you abide in Me, and My words abide in you, ask whatever you wish, and it will be done for you. My Father is glorified by this, that you bear much fruit, and so prove to be My disciples" (NASB). When we abide in Christ, we can come to God in prayer, and whatever we ask will be done for us. That is exciting news!

If we are truly abiding in Christ and His word, we will not wish for selfish, sinful, prideful things, but rather godly opportunities and blessings. This is not to say that we will all walk around in sackcloth with nothing to eat in a humble hut; God says that He is glorified in His generosity to us. We must make sure that we are good stewards of His blessings, always knowing we are blessed to be a blessing, and to give Him credit for all that we have and do. It should be our desire to glorify God in all that we do and say, and that includes our prayers.

I will never forget the day that I sat reeling in the doctor's office with the words, "Brain tumor" ringing in my ears. *How could this be? I thought. I have a baby. I am young. I'm a Christian.* When I tried to view it as being caused or justified by anything I was or did, I couldn't comprehend it. But I was not the center of the circumstance—it was not about me. It was only when I set my heart and mind on making God central that I began to gain understanding. I came to recognize that the peace I felt when I should have been overwrought with anxiety and the joy I experienced when the world said I should be in tears were a result of God's love and faithfulness as I prayed to Him through every test, scan, appointment, treatment, disappointment, and victory.

I have wept through my prayers, hardly able to speak or think clearly. I have prayed on my knees with my face in the floor. I have prayed with my arms in the air and while standing, sitting, or lying down. I have whispered, and I have raised my voice. I have even jumped on the bed with great joy, praying out praises and thanksgiving. All of these are acceptable ways to pray.

All those around me at that time—doctors, nurses, lab techs, radiologists, receptionists, other patients, friends, family members, and neighbors—heard me talk about God, the relationship I have with Him, His love, His presence, and His plan. They heard me speak of how He brought me through the first time, second time, and a third time. The story only continues as God and I continue to journey together using this tumor as a ministry tool that I desire to use for His glory.

Don't get me wrong, I beg Him to take it from me, just as Paul asked God to "remove the thorn in his side." And as Paul knew, I know that God's grace is sufficient if He decides that it is not His plan to release me from it. In my prayers, He has given me the strength to say, "God knows what He is doing, He loves me, and so I know what He is doing is good." I would rather continue in pain for His gain than be released at the loss of His glory.

This is the application of prayer: that God be glorified by the faithfulness of His followers' prayers. It is putting feet to our faith. It is lifting up our prayers and then walking in faith that we have been heard by a loving and mighty God who plans on doing something loving and mighty. It is getting out of bed every morning focused on God's plans for the day and not the problems.

We must know God so that we know how to approach Him in prayer and apply the faith of those prayers to our everyday lives. Our prayer time becomes a prayer life when we continually take all that we know about Him and apply it, liberally, through our prayers. God shows the world, not just His followers, His awesomeness when He answers our prayers and we glorify Him when we pray.

Our faith is grown in our relationship with Him. When we learn about Him through His Word, experience fellowship and worship with other believers, listen to teachers and preachers talk about Him, see Him in His creation, and look for Him in the small things of our daily routine, we learn about Him. The big miracles of His forgiveness, healing, and bringing us through our trials also teach us about our Father. He is truly good all the time. May we always see it, and may the world always see it through our lives to His glory.

Lesson Seven:
Pray Without Ceasing

First Thessalonians 5:17 provides us with one final lesson on prayer: "pray continually." Prayer without ceasing is the right amount of application that we need and God desires.

In all times, in all ways, we need to be in prayer. Whether we are praising Him, thanking Him, confessing our sins, proclaiming His goodness, sharing our hurts or happiness, we need to pray. Pray when you feel that God is prompting you, when He brings someone to your mind or a situation to your attention. Pray through heartache or when you receive your heart's desire. Pray when you see Him in His creation or when you need to be reminded that He is in control. Pray through any and every emotion and situation that comes your way. From your first thought in the morning to the last thought of the day, pray.

CHAPTER FOURTEEN

THE WARRIOR: ANSWER THE CALL

JOHN BORNSCHEIN

In the 1950s, Americans were determined to return to our roots as a republic built on biblical principles. The USSR (present-day Russia) was claiming many of the same values as the United States. Thus, we had to set ourselves apart. This dilemma forced us to reexamine who we were as a people and identify the source that united us as the greatest nation on earth. Our firm faith in God was the defining factor, and Congress agreed, establishing an annual National Day of Prayer in 1952. Two years later, the words "under God" were added to the Pledge of Allegiance, and in 1956, "In God We Trust" was adopted as our national motto.

But in 1962, prayer was removed from public schools. Less than a decade after a series of major victories, the enemy hit us where it hurt—our children. That year, the U.S. Supreme Court ruled against official prayer in public schools, opening the floodgates to a completely secular approach to public education in subsequent years:

- Voluntary prayer was forbidden.
- Inclusion of Scripture was terminated.
- Classes on religion were halted.
- The Bible was eradicated from school libraries.
- Displays of the Ten Commandments were removed in 1980.

- Religious artwork was covered.
- Religious content in student papers or speeches was forbidden.
- The Bible was prohibited in classrooms.

So what happened as a result?

- SAT scores plummeted.
- American high school students regularly finished last, or near the bottom, in math and science testing.
- The United States now ranks 65th in the world in literacy, when only a few decades ago we had one of the world's highest literacy rates.
- Crime in public schools and throughout the nation has escalated.
- Pregnancy rates in schools skyrocketed.[1]

Gatherings of corporate repentance and humility before God are part of America's Judaeo-Christian heritage. Since 1789, the president of the United States has called the nation to prayer more than 134 times.[2] Just as the sons of Issachar understood the signs of the times and sought the Lord's wisdom for the course to take as a nation (1 Chr 12:32), Christian leaders in America need to call the people back to the foundations of the faith. A solemn assembly is needed today more than ever. The cultural landscape is changing dramatically, and the negative impact to the family could have generational consequences. As E.M. Bounds wrote, "We need the spirit of Sunday carried over to Monday and continued until Saturday."[3] This can only be accomplished by leaders who pray.

The prophet Joel (850 BC) called the nation of Israel to assemble and "return to the LORD your God" (Joel 2:13). When a nation faces turbulent times and obstacles that seem insurmountable, there is no more important time to seek the Lord. In 1974, church leaders united in Lausanne, Switzerland, and again in 1989 in Manila, the capital of the Philippines, to refocus and realign the evangelical community in obedience to the Great Commission.[4] Now the National Prayer Committee is calling for leaders to unite as never before in prayer on behalf of America, seeking transformation and healing (2 Chr 7:14).

As E.M. Bounds stated in his powerful book, *The Weapon of Prayer*:

> These days of ours have sore need of a generation of praying men, a band of men and women through whom God can bring His great and His greatest movements more fully into the world. The Lord our God is not straitened within Himself, but He is straitened in us, by reason of our little faith and weak praying. A breed of Christian is greatly needed who will seek tirelessly after God, who will give Him no rest, day and night, until He hearken to their cry. The times demand praying men who are all athirst for God's glory, who are broad and unselfish in their desires, quenchless for God, who seek Him late and early, and who will give themselves no rest until the whole earth be filled with His glory.[5]

Now is the time to stand firm and arise as the Christian soldier you have been called to be. Don't let fear hold you back. God can use you right now—today. You lack nothing that He can't provide.

IMAGE OF A WARRIOR

Let me paint a picture for you of the kind of warrior God uses in His army. Moses was a Levite, born around 1526 BC. Approximately 430 years passed from the time God gave His covenant promise to Abraham to the time He enacted the law through Moses (Gal 3:17). Moses played one of the most vital roles in the redemption of humanity. As the administrator and enforcer of the law, he enacted a system that would not be fulfilled until 1,550 years later by God's perfect design. But Moses wasn't so willing to assume this role (similar to many of us who are called into ministry).

From birth, Moses had been selected by God to save the nation of Israel and lead the people into the promised land. In Exodus 2, all of the Hebrew male infants were taken from their families and brutally thrown into the Nile River to drown. God saved Moses, though, who was taken into Pharaoh's palace to be raised as royalty. But Moses rejected his lofty position because he identified with and cared for his people. One day after witnessing an Egyptian abuse a fellow Hebrew, Moses killed the Egyptian and buried his body in the sand (Exod 2:11–12). When Pharaoh heard of this, he sought to kill Moses, but Moses escaped to the land of Midian.

Soon after he arrived in Midian, Moses came to the rescue of the daughters of Jethro, who were tending their father's flock and had been driven away from a local well by some troublesome shepherds. By now, we have a sense that Moses was frustrated by injustice and had a heroic nature that got him into trouble. Perhaps he was hotheaded and quick tempered. It is difficult to say for sure, but there is no doubt that Moses had little patience for evil and was quick to take matters into his own hands.

After marrying Zipporah, one of Jethro's daughters, Moses was blessed with a son, Gershom (Exod 2:22). Moses was approximately 40 years old at the time. He had a new home and family, and he made his living tending sheep, as was common for the people of Midian. At this point, God chose to intervene, again, calling Moses to do what had never been done: deliver an entire nation from slavery and oppression. Moses should have been eager to do whatever God asked of him—after all, he owed his very life to God. But as we know from the biblical account, Moses was more than a little reluctant to accept the role God had for him.

One day, while Moses was in the desert tending Jethro's flocks, God spoke to him from a burning bush, reminding Moses of the suffering in Egypt and telling him of His intent to rescue the Hebrews and bring them into the promised land. It was a grand and amazing plan. Then God said, "So now, go. I am sending you to Pharaoh to bring my people the Israelites out of Egypt" (Exod 3:10).

Instead of agreeing to God's plan in humility and obedience, Moses insisted that he was the wrong man for the job, saying, "Who am I, that I should go to Pharaoh and bring the Israelites out of Egypt?" (Exod 3:11). God assured Moses of His presence, promising him a sign, telling Moses His name, and describing the miracles He would perform to make the Egyptians listen. But Moses continued asking questions: "What if they do not believe me or listen to me and say, 'The LORD did not appear to you'?" (Exod 4:1).

At this point, God gave Moses two miraculous signs to perform. First, Moses threw his staff on the ground, and it became a snake. When the Lord commanded him to pick up the snake by the tail, it turned back into a staff. Then Moses placed his hand inside his tunic and when he brought it out again, it had become leprous. But the hand was miraculously restored when he placed it back inside his cloak. God then said that he would enable Moses to turn the waters of the Nile to blood if the people still refused to listen.

But Moses continued with his excuses, replying, "Pardon your servant, Lord. I have never been eloquent, neither in the past nor since you have spoken to your servant. I am slow of speech and tongue" (Exod 4:10). God assured Moses that He would give him the words to speak and teach him what to say, but Moses again tried to convince God that he was not the man for job: "Pardon your servant, Lord. Please send someone else" (Exod 4:13). In anger, God proposed yet another solution: He would have Aaron come alongside Moses to speak for him, but Moses would still perform the miracles God had given him. Moses finally relented, agreeing to obey the Lord's command, and the rest is history.

OVERCOMING WEAKNESS

Why did Moses resist obeying God's command? He was afraid, unwilling to adjust his life to God's plan, and in great doubt of his own ability. But wasn't he also in doubt of *God's* ability? This entire discourse emphasizes God's ability and power; God wasn't asking Moses to perform this feat in his own ability or strength, but to simply be an instrument in God's hand.

Moses was afraid and used his own limitations as an excuse for not being up for the job, but there was an underlining issue here as well: a refusal to trust God or entrust himself to God, and perhaps even some bitterness about the past. Moses had been sure of himself years earlier, thinking he was called to deliver his people, but he did it in his own strength and failed. He might have been a bit angry with God over this because the Lord didn't use him the way he thought He should.

Moses' many excuses could have been a smoke screen—not just for lack of confidence in himself (though that was clearly a factor), but a lack of confidence in God and a refusal to trust Him. First he insisted that he was unworthy, and then he claimed that he lacked authority. Moses was afraid that the people would distrust him, and he used his speech impediments as a crutch. Finally, he just cowered in fear at the prospect of doing this seemingly impossible task, despite the presence of the Lord Himself. He gave one excuse after another:

- self-doubt
- lack of authority
- fear of rejection
- fear of public speaking
- fear of the overall assignment

Each time, God countered these fears with viable solutions. He countered Moses' self-doubt with the assurance that He would be with Moses. He countered Moses' lack of authority with His very name— like a king's signet ring. He countered Moses' fear of rejection by giving him the ability to perform miracles. He countered Moses' fear of public speaking with the assurance that He would be with Moses every step of the way to put the words in his mouth. Finally, he countered Moses' overall fear of the assignment by designating Aaron as his personal assistant, a man who would be his confidant and helper.

The fact that God was speaking to Moses directly was not enough; this recorded dialogue shows us that even the chosen were fearful. They were not machines, impervious to human emotion. Christ Himself suffered from the fear of torture and pain that He would experience on the cross. In the midst of his anguish, He prayed, "Father, if you are willing, take this cup from me" (Luke 22:42). Even Elijah, a mighty prophet of the Lord, was overwhelmed with fear when Jezebel put a bounty on his head. As 1 Kings 19:3–5 states, "Elijah was afraid and ran for his life. … He came to a broom bush, sat down under it and prayed that he might die. 'I have had enough, Lord,' he said. 'Take my life; I am no better than my ancestors.'" In Genesis 32:1–12, we see Jacob trembling in fear in anticipation of meeting his brother, Esau, for the first time since stealing his birthright and blessing. Yet on this same journey, Jacob wrestled fearlessly with the living God and received a blessing.

Hebrews 11, also known as the Faith Chapter, tells of men and women of faith who stood firm in the face of persecution and death, even though they never saw God's promises come to pass in their lifetimes. Yet each of these faithful believers had weaknesses, made mistakes, and experienced fear and other human emotions even though they had faith in God.

GOD'S RUBRIC

The story of Moses reminds us that God often selects men and women who appear unqualified in the eyes of the world to perform great and mighty deeds in His power. Other people probably would not have chosen these individuals because of their weaknesses or limitations. David is an excellent example of this.

When the Israelites demanded a king so they would be like other nations, God appointed the prophet Samuel to select the first king of Israel and directed him to anoint Saul. The Scriptures say that Saul was a head taller than any of the other Israelites (1 Sam 9:1–2). Even Samuel was in awe of his stature and said, "Do you see the man the LORD has chosen? There is no one like him among all the people" (10:24).

But King Saul turned away from the Lord and made decisions that brought God's judgment upon the entire nation (1 Sam 15). So God intervened and selected another king, whose heart was fully committed to Him. He didn't pick the obvious choice, either. First Samuel 16:6–8 records that when Samuel arrived at the home of Jesse (David's father) on God's command, he saw Eliab and thought, "'Surely the LORD's anointed stands here before the LORD.' But the LORD said to Samuel, 'Do not consider his appearance or his height, for I have rejected him. The LORD does not look at the things man looks at. Man looks at the outward appearance, but the LORD looks at the heart.'"

David wasn't even in the room with his brothers at the time. His father, Jesse, thought one of the other seven brothers would make a fine king because they were tall, well spoken, and distinguished looking. They were the perfect specimens—perfect for leadership. But God knew they were not the right ones for the job. Samuel asked Jesse if he had any other sons, and Jesse sent for David. As soon as David entered the room, Samuel anointed him king of Israel. This young shepherd boy would become one of the greatest kings the world has ever known.

God has selected other unlikely people to serve Him. The Apostle Paul told Timothy to stay strong and persevere, adding, "Don't let anyone look down on you because you are young, but set an example for the believers in speech, in conduct, in love, in faith and in purity" (1 Tim 4:12). Timothy probably struggled with issues of authority first as a young pastor, he had to teach and reprimand older men. Paul sensed these fears and affirmed him. It is no wonder that Paul wrote,

> Brothers, think of what you were when you were called. Not many of you were wise by human standards; not many were influential; not many were of noble birth. But God chose the foolish things of the world to shame the wise; God chose the weak things of the world to shame the strong. He chose the lowly things of this world and the despised things—and the things that are not—to nullify the things that are, so that no one may boast before him. (1 Cor 1:26–29)

Even the disciples that Christ hand-picked were looked down upon because they were not educated men. But because they had no personal claim to their knowledge or authority, they were able to exalt Christ and His authority in their testimony about Him. Their weakness was their strength.

The point is this: when Moses laid his fears before the Lord, he was speaking on our behalf. Each of us would have trembled as well at the Lord's assignment. Moses was just bold enough (or scared enough) to voice what we ourselves would have felt. The same is true for other biblical heroes. They all had fears and doubts, but God was their strength and confidence. When we look at their accomplishments, we know that God was the source of their power, not their education, their heritage, their wealth, or their stature.

If God could use these men, He can use us. In Christ, we are cleansed and forgiven, thoroughly equipped through the Holy Spirit to do mighty things for God.

RISE TO THE CHALLENGE

Did you know there are more than 300,000 Bible-believing churches in America, as well as 480 dedicated prayer ministries? (That is almost 10 prayer ministries per state.)[6] There are plenty of resources to get the job done, and the harvest is ripe. This is an exciting time in ministry because economic challenges mean that we have to work together. But if we are not intentional, we will lose all the ground won for us by the saints who have given their very lives for the religious freedoms we have today—just as we did in 1962. God has called each of us to be watchmen on the wall for such a time as this. Are we complacently resting on the laurels of our patriarchs and matriarchs, or are we running with the torch that has been handed to us to bring light to a dark world? Stand in the gap on the front lines of the battle! God can change a nation through you.

How do we advance from here? What can we do as the chosen people of God? We can pray without ceasing. We can refuse to abdicate our responsibility and instead ask the Father for the courage of Elijah and Daniel. We can ask for the boldness of Peter and hold up the arms of our fellow soldiers, just as Aaron and Hur held up the arms of Moses (Exod 17:11–12), for the victory is ours in Christ Jesus. We must hold the line!

Forge ahead, confident that you are a son or daughter of the King of kings! In faith and in the power of the Holy Spirit, you can move mountains. Be specific and watch God do an awesome work through you. And as you engage in the battle on the front lines, let Psalm 91 remind you that the Lord Himself is our warrior:

> Whoever dwells in the shelter of the Most High
>   will rest in the shadow of the Almighty.
> I will say of the Lord, "He is my refuge and my fortress,
>   my God, in whom I trust."
> Surely he will save you from the fowler's snare
>   and from the deadly pestilence.
> He will cover you with his feathers,
>   and under his wings you will find refuge;
>   his faithfulness will be your shield and rampart.
> You will not fear the terror of night,
>   nor the arrow that flies by day,

nor the pestilence that stalks in the darkness,

    nor the plague that destroys at midday.

A thousand may fall at your side,

    ten thousand at your right hand,

    but it will not come near you.

You will only observe with your eyes

    and see the punishment of the wicked.

If you say, "The LORD is my refuge,"

    And you make the Most High your dwelling,

no harm will overtake you,

    no disaster will come near your tent.

For he will command his angels concerning you

    to guard you in all your ways;

they will lift you up in their hands,

    so that you will not strike your foot against a stone.

You will tread up on the lion and the cobra;

    you will trample the great lion and the serpent.

"Because he loves me," says the LORD, "I will rescue him;

    I will protect him, for he acknowledges my name.

He will call on me, and I will answer him;

    I will be with him in trouble,

    I will deliver him and honor him.

With long life will I satisfy him

    and show him my salvation."

The battle belongs to Him, and only in His power can we be victorious!

PRAYER

Heavenly Father, as Your servant I will go where You lead me. I dare not build the house without Your blessing, without You as my Rock, my Foundation. Direct my path, O Lord, and make clear the way in which I should journey. I have a deep burden for my neighbors, my community, and even my nation. My heart aches for what You must see. We have lost our way and have thrown dirt on Your mirror. Help me, Father, to unite your people and lead them in life-changing prayer. Help us to understand the relationship you had with Enoch and walk in Your ways.

Truly, Father, I long to know you better. My soul thirsts for you. Give me a courage and passion that are contagious. Give me the words to speak and the tools to equip others. I know money is no barrier to you. I need only to cast my line into the water and draw up a fish to find the coin needed. Give me that faith. Help me to trust you when I am weak and tired. Please bring an Aaron alongside me to keep me lifted up when my heart is faint. At times I feel alone, but as you told Elijah, I know there are others whose hearts are committed to you.

Father, I humbly ask that you would bring people with a love for holiness into my life. May they have your heart to bring people together on holy ground. I need help and resources, my Lord. Prepare me for what you are about to do. Refine and cleanse me so that I may be your instrument. I depend on you for all things, and I thank you for all you have provided. If you give me five talents, I shall make it five more with your favor and blessing. In the name of Jesus, I pray, amen.

ENDNOTES

1. David Barton, *America: To Pray or Not to Pray?* (Aledo, TX: Wallbuilder Press, 1994), 58, 88. Used with permission.

2. American Presidency Project, http://www.presidency.ucsb.edu/ws/index.php.

3. E.M. Bounds, *The Weapon of Prayer* (New Kensington, PA: Whitaker House, 1996).

4. "The Lausanne Covenant," The Lausanne Movement (1974), www.lausanne. org/covenant; "The Manila Manifesto," The Lausanne Movement (1989), www.lausanne.org/all-documents/manila-manifesto.html (accessed October 12, 2010).

5. E.M. Bounds, *The Weapon of Prayer.*

6. Data compiled by Williams Direct, "Churches and Clergy," www.churchladies. com/breakdown.pdf.

FOR FURTHER STUDY

FEED THE SPIRIT

John 3:16

John 14:6

Romans 5:8

Romans 6:23

2 Corinthians 4–5

Philippians 4:13

Titus 3:5

James 1:12

Revelation 3:21

DRIVE THE MIND, DIRECT THE BODY

Exodus 20

Psalm 118:8–9

Proverbs 3:1–7, 21–26

Proverbs 7:1–4

Proverbs 16:3–7

Proverbs 24:10–12

Ecclesiastes 3:1–8

Matthew 4:4

Matthew 5:16

Mark 16:15–16

John 14:15, 23

Romans 12:1–2, 9–21

1 Corinthians 9:27

1 Corinthians 12:12–27

Ephesians 4:29

Philippians 2:3

Colossians 3:23

1 Thessalonians 5:22

1 Timothy 4:7–8

Hebrews 3:14

Hebrews 13: 15–16

1 John 5:14–15

TAKE COURAGE! BE FOCUSED AND CONFIDENT IN HIM

Deuteronomy 31:6

Joshua 1:6–7

2 Samuel 10:12

2 Chronicles 32:7–8

Psalm 56

Isaiah 26:3–4

Acts 4:13

Hebrews 3:6

Hebrews 10:35–36

RECOMMENDED MINISTRIES

ALLIANCE DEFENSE FUND

www.alliancedefensefund.org

The Alliance Defense Fund (ADF) works with other groups to confront the ACLU and other like-minded organizations to keep the door open for the gospel in America. In addition, it is their goal to restore religious freedom as it was originally envisioned by the framers of the U.S. Constitution.

AMERICAN CENTER FOR LAW AND JUSTICE

www.aclj.org

The American Center for Law and Justice (ACLJ) is a public-interest law firm committed to ensuring the ongoing viability of constitutional freedoms in accordance with the principles of justice outlined in Scripture. As a public-interest law firm, the ACLJ is dedicated to the concept that freedom and democracy are God-given, unalienable rights that must be protected both domestically and internationally.

CALVARY FELLOWSHIP CHURCH

www.calvaryfountain.com

The mission of Calvary Fellowship Fountain Valley is to implement teaching and fellowship designed to help God's people establish a firm foundation of faith—to inform, mobilize and equip to reach out locally and impact globally. John Bornschein serves as the senior pastor.

CHRISTIAN LEGAL SOCIETY
www.clsnet.org

The Christian Legal Society's mission is to "inspire, encourage, and equip lawyers and law students, both individually and in community, to proclaim, love, and serve Jesus Christ through the study and practice of law, the provision of legal assistance to the poor, and the defense of religious freedom and [the] sanctity of human life." As a national grassroots network, the society also advocates biblical conflict resolution and public justice.

FACE FOR EDUCATORS
www.prayingeducator.org

Fellowship and Christian Encouragement (FACE) for Educators is an interdenominational Christian ministry serving public, private, and home educators. FACE is one of the fastest growing Christian ministries in the United States, with prayer chapters motivating and encouraging educators throughout the United States and around the world.

THE GLOBAL DAY OF PRAYER
www.globaldayofprayer.com

Each year, on Pentecost Sunday, millions of Christians from 220 nations unite in prayer. The event begins with 10 Days of Prayer followed by 90 Days of Blessing. Having "laid the foundation to saturate nations in prayer," organizers hope to "facilitate a lifestyle of prayer" among smaller groups of people worldwide.

HARVEST PRAYER MINISTRIES

www.harvestprayer.com

Harvest Prayer Ministries (HPM), established in 1993, encourages local churches to pray for revival and world evangelization. HPM believes that God's purposes and plans for His Church can only be established on a foundation of prayer. The ministry's core mission is to "transform lives by teaching prayer" and to "equip the local church to become a House of Prayer for all nations."

INTERCESSORS FOR AMERICA

www.ifapray.org

Founded in 1973, Intercessors for America seeks God's intervention in governmental and cultural issues through fasting and prayer. The ministry not only keeps believers informed about current issues, but also encourages and equips them to intercede for America.

MILITARY MINISTRY OF CAMPUS CRUSADE

www.militaryministry.org

Campus Crusade joins with active and reserve military personnel, commanders, chaplains, and volunteers "to help military men and women and their families in all nations gain spiritual readiness for life and their mission." They believe that "no one should have to go into harm's way without being totally ready in every way: not just physically and mentally, but also spiritually."

THE NATIONAL DAY OF PRAYER

www.nationaldayofprayer.org

The National Day of Prayer is an annual observance held on the first Thursday of May, inviting people of all faiths to pray for the nation. It was created in 1952 by a joint resolution of the United States Congress and signed into law by President Harry S. Truman. More than 40 thousand Christian events are organized annually across the country by the National Day of Prayer Task Force, led by Mrs. Shirley Dobson.

NATIONAL PASTORS' PRAYER NETWORK

www.nppn.org

The National Pastors' Prayer Network (NPPN) connects believers to God through prayer. The network also gathers pastors and prayer leaders together to pray for one another, their congregations, and communities across America and the world as they labor together to fulfill the Great Commission.

NATIONAL PRAYER COMMITTEE

www.nationalprayercommittee.com

The National Prayer Committee (NPC) fosters a number of projects, including the National Day of Prayer, the Nationally Broadcast Concert of Prayer (NBCOP), *Pray!* online magazine, the National Concert of Prayer, and the Denominational Prayer Leaders Network.

PRAY! ONLINE MAGAZINE

www.navpress.com/pray

Pray! is published by NavPress and is the official magazine of America's National Prayer Committee. The magazine keeps believers informed about what God is doing in the Prayer Movement, challenges them to grow in their prayer lives, and offers practical help and encouragement to increase their passion for prayer. No individual with a heart for intercession should be without *Pray!*

THE PRESIDENTIAL PRAYER TEAM

www.presidentialprayerteam.com

The independent, nonprofit organization behind the Presidential Prayer Team has a singular purpose: to encourage specific nationwide prayer for the president of the United States, as well as America, national leaders, and members of the military. The goal is to enlist at least 2.8 million participants, or one percent of the American population, to make this prayer commitment.

RECOMMENDED RESOURCES

Blackaby, Henry, and Norman Blackaby. *Experiencing Prayer with Jesus: The Power of His Presence and Example.* Sisters, OR: Multnomah, 2006.

Bounds, E.M. *E.M. Bounds on Prayer.* New Kensington, PA: Whitaker House, 1997.

———. *The Weapon of Prayer.* New Kensington, PA: Whitaker House, 1996.

Christenson, Evelyn. *Praying God's Way.* Eugene, OR: Harvest House, 2003.

Crawford, Dan R., comp. *Giving Ourselves to Prayer.* Terre Haute, IN: PrayerShop Publishing, 2009.

Dean, Jennifer Kennedy. *Heart's Cry: Principles of Prayer.* Birmingham: New Hope Publishers, 2007.

DeStefano, Anthony. *Ten Prayers God Always Says Yes To: Divine Answers to Life's Most Difficult Problems.* New York: Doubleday, 2007.

Dobson, Shirley. *Certain Peace in Uncertain Times: Embracing Prayer in an Anxious Age.* Carol Stream, IL: Tyndale, 2008.

Fenner, Chris, comp. *Prayers of the Bible for Today.* Katy, TX: Victory Publishing, 2009.

Hartley III, Fred A. *Prayer on Fire: What Happens When the Holy Spirit Ignites Your Prayers.* Colorado Springs: NavPress, 2006.

Helms, Elaine. *Prayer 101: What Every Intercessor Needs to Know.* Birmingham: New Hope Publishers, 2008.

Jeremiah, David. *The Prayer Matrix: Plugging into the Unseen Reality.* Sisters, OR: Multnomah, 2004.

Sproul, R.C. *The Prayer of the Lord.* Lake Mary, FL: Reformation Trust Publishing, 2009.

ABOUT THE AUTHORS

JOHN BORNSCHEIN

John is the executive director of the National Day of Prayer Task Force and an executive member of the National Prayer Committee. During his 17 years in ministry, John has engaged in a vast range of responsibilities, including serving as a missionary and youth pastor, as well as with Mission of Mercy, In Touch Ministries, Focus on the Family, and the National Day of Prayer Task Force.

He and his task-force team have been charged by Mrs. Shirley Dobson to mobilize the Christian community to intercede for America and its leadership in the seven centers of power: government, military, media, business, education, church, and family.

John is the executive producer of *Drive Thru History: America*, the latest video curriculum in the popular series presented on History International and Trinity Broadcasting Network. John has been a frequent speaker with Focus on the Family over the years, including the Spiritual Growth of Children conferences, which are attended by thousands around the country.

As an author, John has contributed to dozens of resources, including the books *Heal Our Land, The Compassion Revolution, Start Your Family, Together in Prayer, Celebration Parenthood* (forthcoming) and *4 Life* (forthcoming). In addition, he has written for several publications, including *Horizons* magazine and *Focus on the Family* magazine. John is a frequent guest on radio and television programs across the nation and has hosted the *Focus on the Family* broadcast and *Life Today* on Salem Communications networks.

In addition, John is the Senior Pastor of Calvary Fellowship Fountain Valley, holds a bachelor's degree in theology and is currently pursuing a Master of Divinity degree from Bethany Baptist Seminary. He has served at the United Nations in New York City and with congressional leaders in Washington D.C. as a representative for the National Day of Prayer. But his true joy is his wife and their five children, who love the Lord. John and his family reside in Colorado Springs, Colorado.

DAVID BUTTS

David received a bachelor of arts degree from Lincoln Christian College in 1975 and bachelor's (1978) and master's (1982) degrees from Indiana State University. He served as associate minister at several Terre Haute churches before moving to Kansas, Illinois, in 1982 to become senior minister of Kansas Christian Church. It was in Kansas that David's passion for prayer and missions began to develop. Today, David is the President of Harvest Prayer Ministries, an organization that works across denominational lines to "equip the local church to become a House of Prayer for all nations." He has served, and continues to serve, in numerous leadership capacities and on boards of directors and committees, including America's National Prayer Committee as chairman, the Denominational Prayer Leaders Network as secretary and treasurer, Pioneer Bible Translators as chairman of the board of directors, and Mission America Coalition as a member of the executive committee.

David has authored articles on prayer and missions for several magazines, including *Christian Standard, The Lookout, Horizons*, and *Pray!* He is the author of *The Devil Goes to Church, Pray Like the King* (with wife, Kim), and *Asleep in the Land of Nod.* He has also completed a videotape presentation on "Leadership for a Praying Church."

KATHY BRANZELL

Kathy is the founder, president, and CEO of Fellowship and Christian Encouragement (FACE) for Educators, which is an interdenominational Christian ministry serving public, private, and home educators. FACE is one of the fastest growing Christian ministries in the United States, with prayer chapters motivating and encouraging educators throughout the United States and around the world. Kathy also manages an independent educational consulting and speaking practice. She is a member of America's National Prayer Committee and a founding member of the Mission America Public School Ministries Coalition and IAM4schools.com, where she worked on special projects with Secretary of Education Rod Paige and President George W. Bush's Office of Faith-Based and Community Initiatives.

Kathy also partners with the Luis Palau Evangelistic Association and travels throughout the United States to assist in hosting the Great Music! Good News! festivals educator brunch. Her focus is on the encouragement and improvement of teachers, children, educational leadership, and those who support the educational process. Kathy can also be heard daily on New Life Radio stations, giving encouragement during her one-minute "Lesson Plan for Life" devotionals.

Prior to assuming her present positions, Kathy served on North Carolina Governor Jim Hunt's educational commission, Smart Start. Kathy was a grant-management consultant and was responsible for evaluating childcare facilities, technical assistance, and educator training. Her efforts contributed to millions of dollars in federal and state funding to central North Carolina education programs. During this period, she also served as an adjunct professor at Fayetteville Technical Community College and conducted motivational and subject matter workshops at numerous colleges, churches, schools, and professional conferences. In 1995 and 1996, she served as an instructor for the Early Childhood Development Program at the University of Georgia, Athens, and from 1992 to 1994 she worked as Regional Trainer and Curriculum Developer at KinderCare in Chicago, Illinois. From 1988 to 1992, she held numerous educational positions, including Head Start instructor, special needs instructor, and kindergarten teacher.

Kathy attended the University of Georgia, Athens, where she received a bachelor of education degree in 1990, with a specialization in early childhood education and child development. She is married to her childhood sweetheart, Russell, and is the proud mother of two children, Chandler and Emily Sara.

DION ELMORE

Dion is a visionary leader and an advocate of developing unique, self-sustaining ministry outreaches through the local church into the local community. These outreaches and organizations connect with individuals and families who may not otherwise come into a local church.

Prior to entering full-time pastoral ministry, Dion was a leader in both corporate and small-business environments, specializing in development, marketing, and advertising. He also served for several years with Focus on the Family and was a leader in the development and marketing of films, books, magazines, and radio dramas, including the Adventures in Odyssey series. He also was involved in Focus on the Family's international efforts, working to establish ministry outreaches in the United Kingdom, Australia, New Zealand, and South Africa.

Dion lives in Colorado Springs, Colorado with his wife, Ann, and their children, Sarah, Rachel, Hannah, and Caleb.

BRIAN TOON

Brian is a retired Navy captain with 25 years of leadership experience. He has a proven track record leading large organizations, including a nuclear-warfare command center, aircraft carrier air and flight-deck operations, and a naval aviation squadron. He has a master of business administration (MBA) from the University of Nebraska, Lincoln, a master's degree in National Security and Strategic Policy from the Naval War College in Newport, Rhode Island, and a bachelor's degree in Business Administration from the University of Colorado, Boulder. An excellent communicator, Brian has participated in numerous interviews on national television networks, including CNN, MSNBC, and ABC, and has been interviewed by the *Los Angeles Times* and *Detroit Free Press*. He has also been featured on the British Broadcasting Corporation network (BBC) while serving as Air Boss on the aircraft carrier *Abraham Lincoln* during Operation Iraqi Freedom. Brian is married and has four children and two grandchildren.

Did you enjoy *The Front Line*?

You can get the digital copy for $2.99 on Vyrso.com!
Use coupon code: **FRNTLN299**

While you're there, check out these other titles on prayer!

Prayers for People under Pressure

A collection of prayers and reflections, this book offers stressed readers paths for their spiritual journey.

Transforming Prayer

This book teaches readers how to connect with God in a way that equips them with practical tools for their prayer life.

Life on Fire

With this book, believers see how living a radically committed, passionate, and purposeful life in Christ is both possible and fulfilling.

Learn more about prayer.

Vyrso.com/Pray • 1-800-875-6467 (U.S.) • +1 360-527-1700 (Int'l)

 Vyrso

CPSIA information can be obtained at www.ICGtesting.com
Printed in the USA
LVOW01s1114060314

376268LV00002B/2/P